Silk Scents & Spice

TRACING THE WORLD'S GREAT TRADE ROUTES

THE SILK ROAD	THE SPICE ROUTE	THE INCENSE TRAIL

UNESCO Publishing / Economica

SILK SCENTS & SPICE

Written by John Lawton
Photographed by Nik Wheeler, Tor Eigeland and Bill Lyons

  UNESCO | **ECONOMICA**

The designations employed and the presentation of material throughout this publication do not imply the expression of any opinion whatsoever on the part of UNESCO concerning the legal status of any country, territory, city or area or of its authorities, or concerning the delimitation of its frontiers or boundaries.

The authors are responsible for the choice and the presentation of the facts contained in this book and for the opinions expressed therein, which are not necessarily those of UNESCO and do not commit the Organization.

Published in 2004 by the
United Nations Educational,
Scientific and Cultural Organization
7, Place de Fontenoy 75352 Paris 07 SP

Designed by Keenan Design Associates, London
Printed by Policrom, Barcelona

ISBN UNESCO 92-3-103927-X
ISBN Economica 2-7178-4951-3

Printed in Spain

BANDA ACEH, INDONESIA'S WESTERNMOST REGION AND FIRST LANDFALL OF EASTBOUND TRADERS IN SOUTH EAST ASIA AFTER THEY CROSSED THE INDIAN OCEAN.

SILK
SCENTS
& SPICE

CONTENTS

Map of Silk, Scents and Spice Routes   8

THE SILK ROAD   11

The Royal Road   15

The Golden Road   25

Mountain Passage   37

The Steppe Route   51

The Imperial Highway   65

THE SPICE ROUTE   75

The Red Sea   79

The Arabian Sea   87

The Indian Ocean   99

The Spice Islands   107

Spice Glossary   114

THE INCENSE TRAIL   117

Index   124

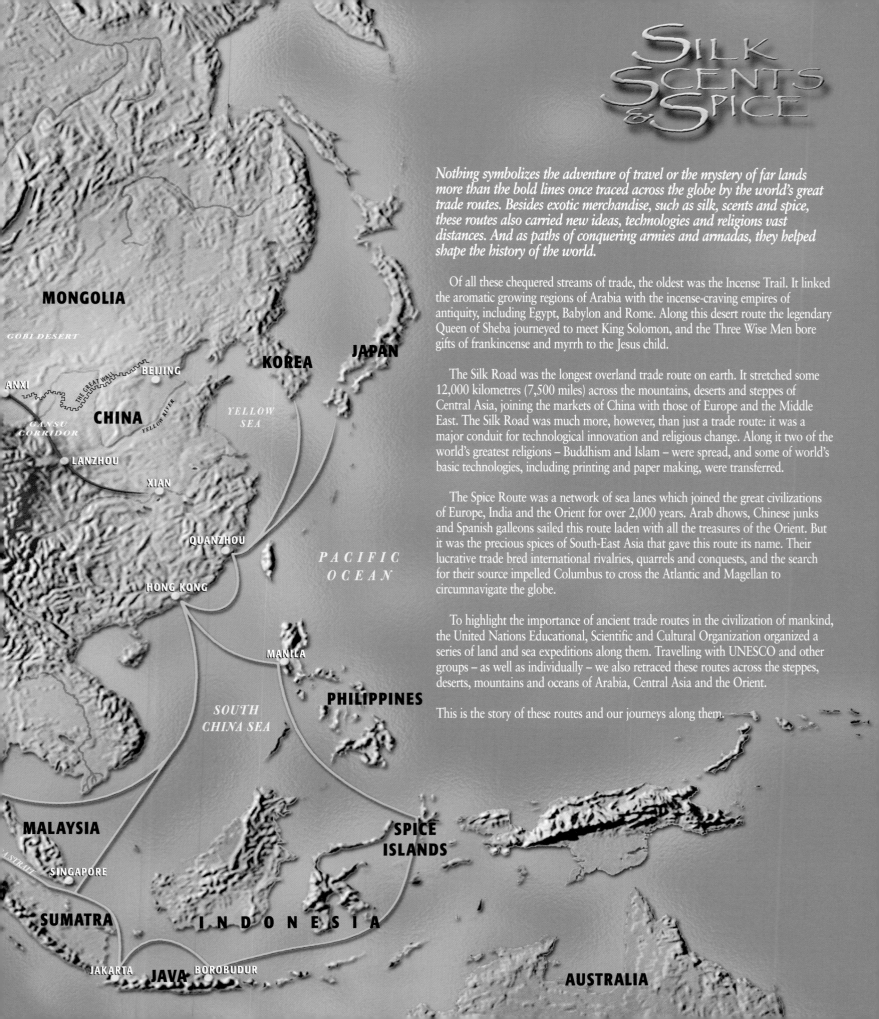

SILK SCENTS & SPICE

Nothing symbolizes the adventure of travel or the mystery of far lands more than the bold lines once traced across the globe by the world's great trade routes. Besides exotic merchandise, such as silk, scents and spice, these routes also carried new ideas, technologies and religions vast distances. And as paths of conquering armies and armadas, they helped shape the history of the world.

Of all these chequered streams of trade, the oldest was the Incense Trail. It linked the aromatic growing regions of Arabia with the incense-craving empires of antiquity, including Egypt, Babylon and Rome. Along this desert route the legendary Queen of Sheba journeyed to meet King Solomon, and the Three Wise Men bore gifts of frankincense and myrrh to the Jesus child.

The Silk Road was the longest overland trade route on earth. It stretched some 12,000 kilometres (7,500 miles) across the mountains, deserts and steppes of Central Asia, joining the markets of China with those of Europe and the Middle East. The Silk Road was much more, however, than just a trade route: it was a major conduit for technological innovation and religious change. Along it two of the world's greatest religions – Buddhism and Islam – were spread, and some of world's basic technologies, including printing and paper making, were transferred.

The Spice Route was a network of sea lanes which joined the great civilizations of Europe, India and the Orient for over 2,000 years. Arab dhows, Chinese junks and Spanish galleons sailed this route laden with all the treasures of the Orient. But it was the precious spices of South-East Asia that gave this route its name. Their lucrative trade bred international rivalries, quarrels and conquests, and the search for their source impelled Columbus to cross the Atlantic and Magellan to circumnavigate the globe.

To highlight the importance of ancient trade routes in the civilization of mankind, the United Nations Educational, Scientific and Cultural Organization organized a series of land and sea expeditions along them. Travelling with UNESCO and other groups – as well as individually – we also retraced these routes across the steppes, deserts, mountains and oceans of Arabia, Central Asia and the Orient.

This is the story of these routes and our journeys along them.

THE SILK ROAD

Fewer names are more evocative of opulence and mystery than the Silk Road, but its actual effect was to demystify. Trade along the route helped create contacts among far-flung countries and cultures, and make things that had been distant and exotic less strange.

The Silk Road formed the first bridge between East and West. It originated 2,000 years ago as a channel of trade in silk and other goods between the ancient empires of China, India, Persia and Rome. But the Silk Road was much more than just a trade route. Above all it was a great channel of communication – a means of contact between peoples and places, and a conduit for the two-way transmission of art, religion and technology. By means of the Silk Road, dialogues were established between diverse peoples, new ideas disseminated and technologies transferred. Meanwhile as the pathway for conquering armies and mass migrations it helped shape the present political, ethnic and religious character of entire regions.

The Silk Road made a major contribution to the civilization of mankind, for besides merchants and their goods there also moved along it the products of human thought, skill and imagination. Craftspeople, scholars, entertainers, adventurers and emissaries from far lands travelled the Silk Road; many languages were spoken, and many cultures blended, in the glittering cities that grew up along it. Inevitably this route formed a cultural causeway carrying new ideas, new philosophies and new artistic styles vast distances.

The expression 'Silk Road' is largely a symbolic one, for although silk gave the route its name, it was not the only cargo carried along it. Nor was it a single 'road' but rather a shifting network of desert trails and mountain tracks that were used more heavily or less as empires and markets flourished or declined, or as merchants sought safer, more practical detours in time of war, plague or famine.

Originating at Xian, the ancient capital of China, one 6,400 kilometre (4,000 mile) route followed the Great Wall westward, skirted the Taklamakan Desert, passed through the Ferghana Valley to the caravan cities of Samarkand and Bukhara, and then around the Caspian Sea to Turkey. Other routes climbed the Pamir Mountains and crossed Afghanistan and Iran to the ports of the eastern Mediterranean, or crossed the Great Wall to Mongolia and traversed the steppes of Kazakstan and southern Russia to Europe. From the main routes subsidiary ones branched out into other networks covering the Middle East, Russia and India. Ports around the perimeter connected land routes with sea routes and stretched the network still farther.

'Thus', wrote Pliny, 'are the ends of the earth traversed – so that Roman women may expose their charms through transparent cloth.'

Both the Roman and Byzantium empires had an insatiable appetite for garments made from silk – so fine that a woman's charms

MODERN TRAFFIC HAS REPLACED PACK ANIMALS ALONG TRACES OF THE SILK ROAD IN NORTHWEST CHINA. BUT THE DEPENDENCE OF EARLIER TRADE ON THE BACTRIAN CAMEL IS EVIDENCED BY CERAMIC MODELS FOUND IN CHINESE IMPERIAL TOMBS.

© BEN JANSSENS

were visible through five layers of them. Roman scholars inveighed against their use, and politicians deplored the drain on the exchequer, but the rich continued to buy and buy, exchanging their gold weight-for-weight for silk. Only a fraction of this gold, however, found its way to China, for this was a trade with thousands of intermediaries. The caravan cities along the way were the ones that profited – charging tolls and taxes on every bale of silk that passed through them, hiring out guides and beasts of burden, and providing accommodation for merchants.

Although Chinese silk provided the impetus for East–West trade, extensive commerce in a variety of other goods moved in all directions. As well as silk, camel caravans transported tea, porcelain and lacquerware west, and carried European amber, silver and gold east. From the Middle East came indigo dyes, glassware and fragrant frankincense. India traded pepper, cotton and sandalwood, Siberia furs, and Central Asia war horses.

The Silk Road was much more, however, than just a trade route. Ideas and cultural traditions also flowed in all directions. The two-way transmission of science and technology was part of the reciprocal flow of ideas along the Silk Road. Out of China came paper making, printing and gunpowder – technologies that changed the Western world – while from the West new developments in mathematics, medicine and astronomy spread to China. Islam, beginning in the Middle East, expanded into Central Asia and India, while Buddhism moved from India to China and Japan via the Silk Road. By this route Christianity, Manichaeism and Zoroastrianism spread vast distances from their original homelands – first through the activities of traders themselves, and later by travellers and missionaries.

The diffusion of new faiths and technologies was just part of the general flow of ideas along the Silk Road, which also played a significant role in the development of scholarship and the arts. For each group whose caravans stopped to make its rugged tracts their temporary home contributed to the art created there. Merchants who travelled the Silk Road turned the oases and caravanserai where they met and mingled into points of communication and dialogue. Scholars and craftspeople made their way along the road in pursuit of knowledge of other societies, to which in turn they contributed their own.

This melding of human thought and experience resulted not only from the influences brought by the Silk Road, but also from the powers and peoples that sought to control the rich trade that flowed along it. For by its own wealth, as well as the access it provided to yet greater prizes, the Silk Road attracted a long succession of invaders. In the eighth century, Muslim Arabs swept east along the Silk Road, decisively altering the strength and distribution of world religions in Central Asia, while in the thirteenth century Genghis Khan unleashed the Mongol hordes along the Silk Road, changing the political organization of much of Asia.

Mass migrations which fashioned the ethnic character of vast regions also coincided with existing trade patterns. Starting in the sixth century, Turkic tribes began a westward wave of migrations along the Silk Road that ultimately swamped Central and Western Asia.

Ironically the Romans and the Chinese never did come face to face, and their reciprocal ignorance is one of the anomalies of the Silk Road. The Chinese apparently had not the vaguest idea where Rome was, while the Romans thought silk grew on trees, and was produced by people who were tall, red haired and blue eyed. Trade went on for almost 1,500 years before the first European – Marco Polo – met the first Chinese and brought back an eyewitness account of the country. Then nobody believed him.

The Silk Road threaded its way through many ages. The first was the long period of prehistory, when occasional contacts between migrating peoples resulted in exchanges of goods. Archaeological excavations have produce tantalizing examples of artefacts from far afield. Strands of silk were found in the hair of an Egyptian mummy from about 1000 B.C., and a gold cup with a richly embossed floral design, made somewhere in the

CHINESE SILKS PROVIDED THE IMPETUS FOR EARLY EAST–WEST TRADE, AND ARE STILL ONE OF CHINA'S MAIN EXPORTS.

Hellenistic world, was unearthed in Siberia. But while nomadic tribes moved along paths that would later become the Silk Road, there were no regular patterns of trade.

Real trade began along the geographical traces that were to become the Silk Road as stable societies developed. Lapis lazuli was brought west from Afghanistan to Sumer and Egypt 5,000 years ago, and Assyrian caravans carried tin from Anatolia to Mesopotamia in the second millennium B.C. It was not, however, until the middle of the last millennium B.C. that an organized system of communications was established. In the Middle East, the imperial highways of the Persians joined Mediterranean lands to Central Asia, while Central Asia was linked to India by the roads built by India's Maurya dynasty.

ALTHOUGH NO LONGER IMPORTANT IN WORLD TRADE, THE SILK ROAD REMAINS A BYWORD FOR TRAVEL AND COMMERCE.

The formal opening of the Silk Road to China is usually placed in the late second century B.C., and is attributed to Emperor Wu of the Han dynasty. Wu, who ruled from 141 to 87 B.C., expanded his empire into Central Asia, where his imperial routes and agents connected with the existing routes to the Middle East and India. Chinese silk was soon finding its way through a network of merchants to the luxury markets of Rome.

In the following centuries, the names of the leading actors changed but the basic roles remained the same. In the Mediterranean, the Byzantine Empire replaced Rome; in China, imperial control passed from the Han to the Tang dynasty; and the middle regions were incorporated into the Islamic realm. All three regions were ravaged in the thirteenth century by the Mongols, who established an empire which – for the only time in history – brought the Silk Road under one rule. It was during this period that European merchants – among them Marco Polo – were able, under Mongol protection, to safely traverse the normally unruly steppes, thus establishing direct contact between China and the West for the very first time.

A final dramatic chapter in the history of the Silk Road was written in the fourteenth century by the Turco-Mongol Timurids. Timur, the dynasty's founder, known in the West as Tamerlane, was one of the most successful warriors the world has ever known. In a series of military campaigns, Timur conquered all of Eurasia from the Great Wall of China to the Urals. East–West trade – disrupted by the collapse of the Mongol Empire – resumed again.

Timur's successors, however, lacked the authority of their ancestor, and were unable to hold together the vast steppe empire he had created. Tribes revolted, and political instability again set in – followed by economic depression and cultural decline. Weak and disorganized, Central Asia was no longer capable of playing the role of intermediary that was vital to continued East–West trade. Meanwhile in 1426, in an effort to expunge long years of foreign influence and resuscitate traditional Chinese values, the Ming dynasty closed China's borders. After 1,500 years as a main artery between East and West, the Silk Road was finally cut, preserving during the following centuries only the romance of its name and the vague memory that somehow, long ago, it had been important.

A fascinating new chapter in the history of the Silk Road began recently with the end of the cold war and disintegration of the Soviet Union. Many lands along the route gained independence with the collapse of the USSR, and for the first time in centuries they are welcoming outsiders to sample their unique culture and explore their vast lands.

Although today it has little economic importance in the patterns of world trade, the Silk Road network has become a goal for those seeking the romance of the past. Adventurous travellers are finding the challenge of discovering the faded glories of the Silk Road to be one of the great experiences of modern travel.

The newly independent nations straddling the old Silk Road have reopened land borders and re-established direct links with both East and West. Today, people travel freely across the once-impregnable border between Turkey and Caucasus, formerly members of rival military pacts. At the opposite end of the Silk Road, China has opened a railway linking Xinjiang with Central Asia via Kazakstan. After a break of some 500 years it is now possible to travel the ancient Silk Road from one end to the other again.

THE ROYAL ROAD

Belching smoke, our Silk Road 'special' sped shrieking through the Asian suburbs of Istanbul, past knots of wide-eyed, waving children fascinated by the unusual sight, sound and smell of an enormous, black, coal-fired steam locomotive. It was an exciting start to an extraordinary journey: along the longest 'road' on earth: 9,600 kilometres (6,000 miles) across Turkey, Central Asia and China, from one end of the ancient Silk Road to the other.

MARBLE COLUMNS AT SARDIS, TURKEY, OUTPOST OF THE PERSIAN EMPIRE AND WESTERN TERMINUS OF THE ROYAL ROAD.

Our journey was the stuff that dreams are made of. Trains, jeeps and buses would whisk us – like magic carpets – from season to season, century to century as we traversed Central Asia's sun-scorched deserts and steppes, and struggled through its snow-choked mountain passes and plateaux. En route, we would marvel at majestic ruins of grand palaces and mausoleums of the conquerors who controlled the Silk Road; fortified caravanserais that safeguarded its trade; and magnificent mosques and temples glorifying the religions that spread along it.

This was only the first of a series of journeys along the vast network of ancient trade routes known collectively as the Silk Road. We would also retrace these routes across the Middle East, the Mongolian steppe and worn-torn Afghanistan, as well as travelling the incredible Karakoram Highway to Kashgar.

At the western end of this great highway of human intercourse stood Constantinople, centre – and emporium – of the Christian world. It became the capital of the Roman Empire when Constantine, the empire's first Christian emperor, moved his court there in A.D. 330 to escape decadent Rome. Within 200 years the former Greek trading post – known as Byzantium until Constantine renamed it after himself – had become the most prestigious city in Europe, and for almost a millennium it was the main western terminus of the Silk Road, controlling the supply of silk to European markets. It was here that the widest varieties of types and colours of silken cloth could be found. And it was here that we began our journey.

Although the Silk Roads withered and died, the imperial grandeur of Constantinople – captured by the Turks in 1453 and renamed Istanbul – remains stamped indelibly on its skyline of mosques, towers and palaces, banked magnificently up the hills above the triple confluence of the Bosphorus, the Sea of Marmara and the Golden Horn. The city still owes much of its importance to trade: oil tankers and container ships steam constantly up and down the Bosphorus, which links Russia's Black Sea ports with the Mediterranean, while high overhead, convoys of eighteen-wheeled trucks carrying Middle East-bound cargos rumble over two mile-long suspension bridges linking Europe and Asia.

Theoretically, that is how one goes from Europe to Asia: by simply crossing the Bosphorus. In practice, though, the suburbs on one side are much the same as on the other; the continents overlap and the boundary is a far more subtle one. Somewhere that night, as we trundled across Anatolia, we slipped insensibly into Asia.

TRADITIONAL TURKISH COSTUME.

Anatolia, or Asia Minor, has over the centuries been both bridge and battleground between East and West. The Persians were the first power to

master it all, defeating Cresus, the proverbially wealthy king of Lydia – one of the first rulers to mint his own coins – in 546 B.C. Next, like a great sword-thrust from the west, came Alexander, who crushed the Persians at the battle of Issus in 333 B.C. and occupied the whole of Anatolia in the reverse direction.

Later Rome and Parthia waged a long and bitter struggle over Anatolia. The Romans triumphed in the end, but by the sixth century their rule had given way to that of Byzantium. Then the Arabs, and later the Seljuk Turks, erupted from the East, and Anatolia became the battleground of a new struggle: Christianity versus Islam.

At the battle of Malazgirt, in 1071, the Seljuk Turks defeated the Byzantine armies and occupied central Anatolia. But they too succumbed in turn, to the Mongols. When the Mongol tide ebbed, in the fourteenth century, another tribe of Turks, the Osmanli or Ottomans, suddenly began expanding. They smashed the remnants of Byzantium and established an empire that ultimately stretched from the Adriatic to the Arabian Gulf. It too finally collapsed in the holocaust of the First World War, but the Turks hung on to Anatolia, which together with European Thrace now forms modern Turkey.

It was a fitful first night as we crossed this historic land in the strange

© YAGMUR ACAR

and unsteady surroundings of a train compartment, but we were lapped in luxury compared with the hardships of the traders who once travelled the Silk Road. By day they walked alongside their pack animals – camels, mules, yaks or horses, depending on the terrain – and they slept most nights under the stars. In the mountains, where avalanches could bury an entire caravan, they were prey to frostbite and snow blindness; in the desert, where sandstorms could pin them down for days, they were tormented by heat and thirst.

There were human enemies too: bandits who preyed on the richly laden caravans. For safety the merchants often joined together in convoys, sometimes with as many as 1,000 camels. The richest among them maintained men at arms; the less wealthy would pay for the privilege of being under their protection.

Despite all the differences of detail between their camel caravans and our mechanized one – a powerful locomotive, seven sleeping cars, two restaurant cars, a shower car and two Pullman coaches – the basic rationale behind both was the same: We were travelling in groups for convenience and economy. Our group was making a journey by special train to celebrate the '2,000th anniversary' of the opening of the Silk Roads.

Unlike us, however, few merchants ever made the entire journey along the Silk Road, for trade between China and the Mediterranean was almost always carried out in stages. No individual caravan made the entire journey, and goods changed hands many times before they reached their final destination. Only in the fourteenth century, when the Mongol empire ruled almost the whole length of the Silk Road, were merchants like the Polo family able to make the entire trip.

The meeting of peoples of East and West, the exchange of ideas and technologies, and the transmission of languages and literature, were first made possible by the Persian Achaemenid empire between the sixth and fourth centuries B.C. People were attracted from many points of the compass to the Persian capital, Persepolis (in present-day Iran), along roads built by the emperor Darius to link the far-flung marches of the empire, which stretched from the River Indus to the Aegean Sea.

The most famous of these was the Royal Road, a 2,500 kilometre (1,600 mile) all-weather highway from Susa in Iran, across Mesopotamia and Anatolia to the Aegean Sea. Like modern roads, it bypassed big cities to avoid delays, and although camel caravans took some ninety days to make the journey, relays of royal messengers riding fresh steeds from one fortified station to another could do it in nine. These couriers, wrote Herodotus, were 'stayed neither by snow nor rain nor heat nor darkness from accomplishing their appointed course' – a description adapted as a motto by the United States Postal Service and still invoked today.

Suddenly the world was a smaller place. The enormous extent of the Persian Empire – at its height it included all of the Middle East and Egypt – meant that markets and producers, formerly separated by hostile powers, were now united under a single rule. Over the centuries, the Royal Road became the main trade route across the Anatolian Plateau. It was also the preferred line of march of invading armies.

Following the Royal Road our train climbed steadily upward during the night, depositing us at dawn on the Anatolian Plateau. This is a country of rolling rust-coloured hills and fertile purple and green plains punctuated by compact mud-brick villages and lines of lithe poplar trees. At its centre stands Ankara. Not much more than a primitive country town when Mustafa Kemal Atatürk, founder of modern Turkey, set up headquarters there in 1920, Ankara is now a metropolis of 3.3 million people and capital of modern Turkey.

Ankara has been a natural stronghold since Hittite times, and from its fastness Ataturk turned military humiliation into victory. He repulsed the Greeks who, with British backing, were attempting to recapture what had once been the Anatolian provinces of the Byzantine empire, and restored to his demoralized and dismembered country its independence and its pride.

Today Ankara's ancient citadel and the massive colonnaded yellow limestone mausoleum where Ataturk is buried face each other across the city from atop two small hills. Below, built from twenty-five different varieties of Anatolian marble, stands Turkey's enormous parliament building. It took twenty-one years to construct and was completed in 1960, the very year in which an army coup briefly abolished the parliamentary regime. It was said that the sight of such a stupendous building standing empty prompted the generals to restore democracy more quickly than they might otherwise have done.

Shaving is hazardous on a moving train, so while fellow travellers took a city tour I headed for the railroad station's busy barber's shop. There, buried beneath mounds of white shaving foam, I eavesdropped on fellow customers' views of Turkey's latest political happenings. It all sounded too familiar: I had covered Turkey for many years as a foreign correspondent, and once again, after inclusive elections, party leaders were trying to form a government under the army's watchful eye.

Refreshed and back on board, we followed the Royal Road east – at a pace not much faster than the couriers of the Persian kings. Although we were now pulled by a smart new red and white diesel locomotive, it took us ten hours to cover the 300 kilometres (188 miles) between Ankara and Kayseri, a city that has been a major East–West trading centre since Assyrian times.

The Assyrians, who inhabited northern Mesopotamia in the second millennium B.C., established great trading outposts in Anatolia, which they called *karums*. Among these, the *karum* of the central Anatolian city state of Kanesh, 22 kilometres (14 miles) northeast of Kayseri, was the centre.

Using routes through Kanesh, today known as Kültepe, the Assyrian merchants imported tin and cloth by caravans of 200 to 250 donkeys, and sold their goods to the

indigenous Hittite people for silver and gold. Thousands of Assyrian cuneiform tablets – unearthed in the foreign trading colony built adjacent to the palaces of the princes of Kanesh – provide details of these transactions. From these tablets we also learn the routes taken by traders. Caravans set out from Babylon and, following the course of the Tigris and Euphrates, travelled to Cilicia, and from there to the city of Kanesh and its famous marketplace.

When we attempted to retrace this route several years later we had to turn back. After following the Euphrates for several weeks across Turkey and Syria, we were barred from entering Iraq because of the Gulf War – a reminder that Silk Road merchants too were often forced to take lengthy detours to avoid conflicts.

International trade remained the backbone of the central Anatolian economy until medieval times. To safeguard it, the pragmatic Seljuk sultans and their viziers built a network of caravanserais – fortified inns with accommodation for merchants, their goods and their pack animals – in the thirteenth century. Motels of their time, these castle-like buildings provided safety on the caravan routes as well as halting places for armies on the move. The Persian word 'caravanserai' comes from a root meaning 'to protect'; the Turkish form, *kervansarayi*, means 'caravan palace'. Even today the vast profiles of the caravan palaces punctuate the endless skyline of the Kayseri plain, their large, richly carved portals symbolizing the relief and security they once offered in the midst of a long and hazardous journey.

Along the road between Kayseri and Sivas alone, I counted no fewer than twenty-four caravanserais, including possibly the best example of this type of Seljuk civic architecture: Sultan Han, built in 1232–6 by Sultan Alaeddin Keykubad. On three sides of its courtyard are chambers that served as private bedrooms, storerooms and a bath house. Merchants and their saddle horses were accommodated in a large central hall. The fourth side is occupied by deep, open arcades that housed camels and carts. And in the middle of the courtyard stands a mosque, its surface adorned with beautiful Seljuk stone carving.

Like the medieval merchants who stopped here to rest themselves and their animals, repair their equipment and polish their weapons, we too checked into a hotel in Kayseri to shower, get a sound night's sleep – difficult on a train – and have our laundry done. But the arrival of our large party, all trying to do the same thing at once, overtaxed facilities: elevators seized up, hot water ran out and laundry came back in promiscuous confusion.

With such a large group, mealtimes were also chaotic, and frequently sent photographer Tor Eigeland and me in search of nearby neighbourhood restaurants unaffected by our group presence. In Kayseri we had a delicious lamb kebab covered in fresh yoghurt. We also stocked up on the local delicacy, *pastirma* – dried beef cured in hot spices and coated with a pepper paste – and a bottle of Turkish *raki*, as our contribution to 'corridor parties' – now a nightly affair on our train.

Next morning the Kayseri hotel elevator was working again – after its fashion. 'It's just not stopping at any of the floors', explained one bemused matron as we followed her carefully down the unlit stairs. It was the first of many darkened stairways and precipitous passages we climbed that day, for we visited the subterranean cities and cave churches of the lava-filled basin of Cappadocia. Located

THE ROLLING HILLS AND FERTILE PLAINS OF THE ANATOLIAN PLATEAU, FOR CENTURIES BOTH BRIDGE AND BATTLEGROUND BETWEEN EAST AND WEST.

west of Kayseri between two extinct volcanoes, Cappadocia's soft rock has been fissured by earthquakes and honeycombed by erosion into thousands of crooked pinnacles, like rows of great white whales' teeth many stories high.

Local people named them 'fairy chimneys' because they thought the weird formations were made by magic, and early Christians hollowed out the cones to build more than 200 churches inside. Shaped internally like conventional buildings, with arches and columns apparently supporting vaults and domes, they are in fact spaces cut out of the rock. The Christian community lived in secret underground cities nearby. Invisible from above, the cities comprise a labyrinth of passages, extending as many as eight stories deep into the rock. On both sides of these tunnel 'streets', tiny dwellings, storerooms and communal kitchens were hewn out. In the eleventh and twelfth centuries, thousands of people are thought to have worked and lived there.

Two of the vast underground tenements have been made safe and fitted with electric lights so the adventurous can explore the strange subterranean world of these troglodyte Christians who, for almost 2,000 years, kept their faith and their churches intact, decorating the latter with beautiful frescoes. Now, however, the same erosive process that helped form the churches is slowly destroying them: the rough stone outer walls of the hollowed-out cones are collapsing, leaving their gilded interiors exposed. Without a major international restoration effort these unique churches will simply disappear.

That night fires set by farmers to burn off wheat stubble were spread spectacularly across the hillsides, like the tongues of glowering lava that filled the Cappadocian basin thousands of years ago, long before even the Royal Road coursed across the Kayseri plain en route to the present Turco-Syrian border.

This border was frontier country, too, in Rome's long war with Parthia. And it was here that the Romans – according to the historian Florus – got their first sight of silk. During the battle of Carrhae, in 53 B.C., mounted Parthian archers unfurled brilliantly coloured silk banners, dazzling and terrifying the Roman legionnaries – already disoriented by the Parthians' 'parting shot' tactics of firing as they withdrew – and contributing to their rout.

Within seven years of that event, according to an account written by Dionysius Cassius, silk canopies were used to shelter spectators during Julius Caesar's triumphal entry into Rome. Silk cloth quickly became indispensable in every great Roman household, and soon hundreds of caravans laden with bales of silk were lumbering along the Silk Roads, to satisfy Rome's insatiable demand.

From Kayseri, the Royal Road went southeast to Samasat, where it crossed the River Euphrates, and continued to Harran, near the present Turco-Syrian border. From Harran a branch went south through Palmyra, Damascus and Jerusalem to Memphis in Egypt. The main road went eastwards to Nineveh and thence to Susa, near the head of the Arabian Gulf. Eventually I would take these routes too, but for the moment we were headed northeast toward the Black Sea – one of the principal outlets for silks from the East during the Middle Ages.

FAIRY CHIMNEY ROCK FORMATIONS AT CAPPADOCIA, INSIDE WHICH EARLY CHRISTIANS CARVED OUT FRESCOED CHURCHES.

The 'Silk Road Express', as our mechanized caravan had been dubbed, was making slow progress. Although modern highways and railroads have replaced tortuous caravan trails along the Silk Road, these links too can be tenuous in the face of natural or human forces. The railroad traversing eastern Turkey, for example, is only a single track – and now it was blocked by a derailment far up ahead.

Finally edging past freight cars toppled crazily by the track on the eastern fringe of the Anatolian Plateau, we made the twisting, uphill run to Erzurum: powering between high mountains, weaving alongside tumbling river torrents and bursting out of black tunnels onto shimmering plains. The seasons, as well as the scenery, changed too: here leaves of the ubiquitous poplars were already an autumnal gold, and smoke curled lazily from the chimneys of farmhouses whose flat roofs were piled high with fodder for the fast-approaching winter.

MOUNT ARARAT, LEGENDARY LANDFALL OF NOAH'S ARK, DOMINATES TURKEY'S ROAD LINKS WITH NEIGHBOURING IRAN AND AZERBAIJAN.

Erzurum, situated amid high mountains at 2,000 metres (6,500 feet), was busy too preparing for winter: hundreds of shiny metal stoves were on sale on sidewalks swept by icy winds. In smoky, overheated coffee houses Turks with scrub-brush moustaches drank black tea, a sugar lump held beneath the tongue to sweeten the strong brew.

Unofficial capital of eastern Turkey, Erzurum was once a major caravan crossroads. From there highways radiate northeast through Kars into Georgia and Russia, southeast through Tabriz into Iran, northwest to Trabzon on the Black Sea, southwest through Malatya to the Mediterranean, and due west through Sivas and Ankara to Istanbul. Although today Erzurum's caravanserais serve different purposes – one has been converted into workshops for local jewellers – the city is still a regular watering hole for long-distance truck drivers en route to Iran.

The truckers' route twists through Tahir Pass: 3,000 metres (9,000 feet) at the summit, its steep ice-sheeted roads virtually inaccessible for four months of the year. This route then skirts Mount Ararat – legendary resting place of Noah's Ark – and crosses Dogubeyazit plain, which forms a corridor between Turkey and Iran.

A vast dormant volcano, Mount Ararat towers majestically and mysteriously over the pasture lands of eastern Turkey. Sometimes visible and sometimes not, it is easy to visualize how legends have grown up around it. Many have explored Mount Ararat, in the hope of finding a trace of Noah's Ark. Some have claimed to have seen its remains, and a few have even brought back bits of wood which they professed were part of it. Although no conclusive proof of its existence has ever been found, local legend still maintains that the Ark lies buried beneath the ice cap that permanently covers Ararat's 5,165 metre (16,940 feet) conical peak.

In the bustling border town of Dogubeyazit we ate *assure*, a pulse and nut pudding said to have first been concocted by Noah's wife from the leftovers of all the supplies aboard the Ark. Once an important caravan halt on the Silk Road, Dogubeyazit is still a major staging post for East–West travel and trade, dominated by the imposing Ishak Pasha fortress-palace. Located in the borderlands between ancient Arab, Roman and Persian empires, Ishak Pasha palace is influenced by the architecture of all three. Its Islamic arches, Byzantine pillars and Iranian carved stone portals reflect a synthesis of far-flung artistic styles brought together by converging strands of the Silk Road network.

History has placed Erzurum repeatedly between powers at contention. Formerly a Byzantine outpost guarding against the Turks, Erzurum was for many years an outpost of the Turks against the Soviet Union: headquarters of the Turkish Third Army, protecting NATO's southeast flank against the forces of the Warsaw Pact.

After Turkey joined the western alliance, Moscow made the Caucasian border impregnable, with lines of barbed wire, ploughed strips and guard towers. Even when a chink appeared during the years of *glasnost* (openness), crossing it was a grim experience. Advancing slowly towards the border at night, we passed trains loaded with jeeps, artillery, armoured cars and troops in full battle gear. We awoke the next morning on the edge of no man's land. A layer of freshly fallen snow covered the hills overlooking the frontier. The ruins of an old fortress were silhouetted against the skyline, and barbed-wire fencing, strung between steel watch towers, stretched off into the distance on both sides of the railroad track. There was little sign of human activity. A road across the border was completely overgrown with grass.

A Russian train rolled slowly over the border. The Turkish train moved forward to meet it. They stopped on opposite sides of a platform, and lugging our baggage, we switched from one train to the other. For security reasons, the rail tracks on opposite sides of the border are of different gauges, and so are all the dimensions of the rolling stock. This meant a wobbly climb up a wooden plank from the Turkish-built platform into the Soviet train. Once aboard, we were confined to our sleeping compartments until border formalities were complete. Surly border guards worked their way from compartment to compartment checking passports, counting foreign currency and confiscating literature, while men in blue overalls probed the far corners of each compartment with flashlights.

All this changed with the disintegration of the Soviet Union, of which the now-independent countries of the Caucasus were part. Borders with Turkey were reopened, and trade along traces of the old Silk Road was resumed. Links between relatives on both sides of the border, cut for seventy years, have been restored.

Cone-roofed churches – Armenia and Georgia are traditionally Christian – now replaced the domes and minarets of Muslim Turkey. There were other differences too. Compared with the 'lived in' feel of the Turkish train we had left at the border, the Caucasus rolling stock was new and impersonal, and its passengers somewhat subdued after the tedious frontier crossing. But large quantities of caviar and vodka served by cheerful Georgian waitresses soon had spirits restored. Detraining at Tbilisi, several couples waltzed to the music of a welcoming band – appropriately playing Billy Strayhorn's *Take the 'A' Train*.

Although only a small country, Georgia is richly and diversely endowed with fertile land and contrasting scenery, ranging from the subtropical Black Sea shore to the icy crests of the Caucasus Mountains. It was in Georgia, according to legend, that Jason and the Argonauts found the fabled Golden Fleece, and the capital, Tbilisi, reflects the republic's less mythical economic and cultural riches. Its main streets and squares are dominated by

THE ISLAMIC ARCHES, BYZANTINE PILLARS AND CARVED STONE PORTALS OF ISHAK PASHA PALACE, IN EASTERN TURKEY, REFLECT A SYNTHESIS OF FAR-FLUNG ARTISTIC STYLES BROUGHT TOGETHER BY CONVERGING STRANDS OF THE SILK ROADS NETWORK.

theatres, libraries and academies, and the embankment of the Kura River, which cuts through its centre, is lined with sculpture and statues. Its traditional ornate balconied buildings, clinging to the steep banks of the river, have been tastefully restored, and even the modern housing complexes that spill out over the surrounding hillsides are impressive.

We skipped meals in the crowded, cavernous restaurant of the Iveria Hotel, a soulless multi-storey complex run by the state tourist agency, and ate spicy Georgian sausages instead: lunch at a riverside buffet and dinner in a cheery cellar restaurant, its walls covered with paintings of Tbilisi's favourite cartoon character, a mythical street sweeper created by the Georgian painter Pirosmani.

A Zoroastrian temple at Surakhany in Azerbaijan, from where the religion spread east along the Silk Road to India and is still practised there today.

Marco Polo described Tbilisi, in the thirteenth century, as a 'fine city of great size' where 'silk and many other fabrics' were woven. Most silk reached Tbilisi by way of the Eurasian Steppe route across Kazakstan and southern Russia, and was sent west to the Black Sea – whose ports gave access, via the Bosphorus strait, to the Mediterranean. Genoese merchant sailors pushed into the Black Sea, establishing outposts in the Russian Crimea and at Trabzon in Turkey. Their mighty mercantile fleets enabled them to circumvent the intermediary Muslim powers of the Middle East.

Georgia continues its traditional role as a transit state between Asia and Europe: pipelines carry oil across its territory from neighbouring Azerbaijan to the Black Sea. Forests of derricks and 'nodding donkey' oil pumps lined the rail route we now followed east through what was, until the discovery of petroleum in the Middle East, the world's largest oil field, on the western shores of the Caspian Sea. It is also among the world's oldest: oil has been drawn from its wells since the fifth century. Today over 100 nationalities live in Baku, the capital of Azerbaijan, attracted by work in the oil fields. Their numbers make the city the largest in the Caucasus, its imposing modern buildings rising up the slope of the natural amphitheatre surrounding the Bay of Baku.

A short bus ride from the city, at Surakhany, stands a deserted Zoroastrian temple, its ceremonial fires – which form part of the religion's ritual – still burning. The ancient pre-Islamic religion of Persia, emphasizing the contending forces of evil and good, Zoroastrianism was founded in the sixth century B.C. by the reformist prophet Zoroaster in an attempt to unify worship under one god. It spread east along the Silk Road, and flourished in Sogdiana up to the eighth century, when it was displaced by Islam. The religion is still practised in isolated areas of the world, most notably in India.

Two other religions – Manichaeism, a blend of Zoroastrianism, Buddhism and Christianity, and Nestorianism, a Christian sect whose adherents believed that Jesus was two persons, one human and one divine – also spread to China via the Silk Road. Although always a minority religion, Nestorianism played an important role in the history of the Silk Road. Indeed, it was two Nestorian monks who, in one of the earliest feats of industrial espionage, are said to have smuggled the secret of silk manufacture from China to the West. They concealed silkworm eggs, whose export the Chinese forbade, in hollows in their staffs, and travelled in winter so the eggs would not hatch out.

Although their audacious action revealed the Chinese secret of sericulture and broke the Persian monopoly of the silk trade, it had little effect on economic and cultural exchanges along the Silk Road. By the seventh and eighth centuries, in fact, these exchanges had reached unprecedented heights, principally because of the prosperity and power of the Tang dynasty in the East, the Byzantine Empire in the West, and the Arab hegemony inbetween.

THE GOLDEN ROAD

Few landmarks have tantalized the minds of men more than the legendary caravan cities of Samarkand and Bukhara. Neighbours on the Golden Road trade route across Central Asia, their opulence and beauty fired for centuries the imagination of poets and adventurers.

'For the lust of knowing what should not be known', wrote British poet-diplomat James Elroy Flecker, 'we make the Golden Journey ... to divine Bukhara and happy Samarkand.' Marlowe, Milton and Keats wrote about these cities too – though none of them had been there. In fact, so remote behind their barriers of deserts and mountains were Samarkand and Bukhara that, until quite recently, they were visited only rarely by modern travellers.

During the seventy-five years of Soviet domination, Central Asia and its bewildering mix of peoples were all but forgotten by the rest of the world. The grand palaces and mosques that once graced the Silk Road were eclipsed by miles of gloomy poured-concrete apartment blocks. The only major land routes out of the region were roads and railways that all eventually led to Moscow.

My first visit to Samarkand was hardly 'golden' – it poured with rain. But even leaden skies failed to dim the lustre of the thousands of blue-glazed tiles which cover the city's ancient mosques, mausoleums and *madrasa* (religious colleges). The rain, in fact, seemed to give the tiles added sparkle, while red, green and yellow umbrellas made contrasting colour splashes among the sea of blues.

The Golden Road linked Central Asia with the metropolises of Mesopotamia, and was the hub of the Silk Road network. For centuries ancient caravan trails – from Siberia to India, from China to Europe – converged on the verdant oases of Samarkand and Bukhara. Silks and porcelain from the East, amber and furs from the North, gems and spices from the South, and perfumes and ivory from the West, were bartered, bought and sold in their teeming bazaars.

Huge profits derived from the management of international trade made Samarkand and Bukhara centres of luxury and learning, for ideas too travelled with the merchants and their wares. The first paper mill west of the Great Wall of China operated in eighth-century Samarkand, while the most influential library in the tenth-century Islamic world was the one in Bukhara.

The commercial and cultural vitality of these two cities lured the finest intellects of the time. The brilliant physician Ibn Sina, known in the West as Avicenna, wrote his celebrated *Canon of Medicine* in Bukhara, and the royal astronomer Ulugh Beg, using an enormous sextant set in a hillside overlooking Samarkand, plotted the position of over 1,000 stars. But the city's prosperity and strategic location also attracted a long succession of invaders.

When Alexander the Great marched into Central Asia, Samarkand and Bukhara were already flourishing trade centres. A Macedonian who became steeped in Greek culture after conquering Greece, and then

CHAR MINAR (FOUR MINARET) MOSQUE AT BUKHARA, WHERE ELEVEN CARAVAN TRAILS ONCE CROSSED AND MERCHANTS IN TRADITIONAL STRIPED ROBES CAN STILL BE SEEN TODAY.

25

an oriental monarch captivated by the idealism of the East, Alexander was the embodiment of cultural intermingling. During his time the culture of the Greek world was transmitted into Asia in an unprecedented flow of people and ideas, technologies, artistic trends and architectural formulae. The traffic, however, was not only one-way. Alexander and the scholars who accompanied him met Asian philosophers, whose ideas they took back to Greece along with tributes of gold and artefacts, which enriched the classical world of the West.

Following Alexander's death – he was struck down by fever at the age of 32 – his empire was divided among his generals. One of them, Seleucus, won control of the eastern part and founded the Seleucid dynasty. But within a century the Parthians had overthrown the Seleucides, blocked the eastward advance of the Romans, and established themselves as intermediaries in the lucrative silk trade between China and the West.

When Parthian power waned, first the Kushans and then the Sassanians seized control of Central Asia, until suddenly in the sixth century the Turks burst from their homeland in Mongolia, conquering a vast swathe of steppeland stretching nearly from the Pacific to the Black Sea. By 565 these fierce mounted nomads had extended their sway over most of the main cities of Central Asia, including Bukhara and Samarkand, and controlled the Silk Roads.

The Turks were the first nomad nation to exploit trade. They concluded treaties with the Persian and Byzantine empires, and provided security for caravans traveling across Central Asia. Between the sixth and seventh centuries the Turkic Khanate split into eastern and western segments. Weakened by internecine wars, East Turkistan became a protectorate of the Chinese Sui dynasty, while West Turkistan fell to the Arabs.

The famous Arab general Qutaiba ibn Muslim invaded Central Asia in 705, and within forty years had incorporated most of Central Asia into the Islamic realm. His reign was not without problems. One of them was the beautiful Princess Khatum, Queen Regent of Bukhara. She is said to have fled to Samarkand before the Arab armies, shedding a slipper worth 200,000 *direm* – the most valuable slipper of all time. But she was soon back, leading the people in revolt and re-establishing herself in Bukhara. It was to take three years – from 706 to 709 – and four campaigns before the Bukhariots were finally subdued.

Samarkand too changed hands on several occasions, finally falling to Qutaiba in 711. Legend relates that on the arrival of his forces outside Samarkand, the inhabitants shouted from the wall that they were wasting their time. 'We have found it written', they cried, 'that our city can only be captured by a man named "Camel Saddle".' Being ignorant of Arabic they did not know that 'Qutaiba' meant exactly that.

Following in Qutaiba's footsteps, we crossed the once-mighty Oxus River – now renamed the Amu Darya and almost run dry from wasteful irrigation – and drove across the unrelenting Kara Kum (Black Sands) Desert joining Turkmenistan and Uzbekistan. When central authority over the trade routes was lacking, fierce Turkmen raiders ranged freely over the Kara Kum, charging from their lairs in the mountainous borderlands shared with Iran and Afghanistan to ambush richly laden caravans. They rode long-backed, long-necked Akhal-teke horses, which possessed great stamina and a loping pace that could be kept up for hours on a raid, or *chepow*. Although deprived of the excitement of the *chepow* today, the Turkic people still raise this special breed of horse for racing.

The Arabs' conquest of Central Asia put them on a collision course with China, which was in a period of vigorous expansion of its own. The two superpowers met for the first and only time at Talas in 751. The epic battle to determine which of the two civilizations –

Arab or Chinese – would dominate Central Asia lasted five days, with the two titans attacking, retreating, reforming and attacking again inconclusively, until finally, joined by the mounted bowmen of the Qarluq Turks, the Muslim Arabs won the day.

Chinese chronicles say the Turks treacherously changed sides in the midst of the action, attacking them from the rear, but Arab historians claim the Turks had been secretly allied with them all along, and that the attack from behind was part of a carefully prearranged battle plan. Whatever the case, the Chinese army broke and fled, leaving the Arabs to rule Central Asia for the next 200 years.

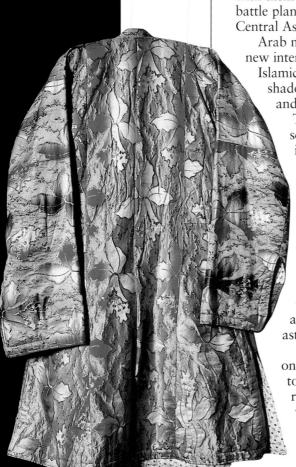

Arab merchants established direct contact with China, and by the ninth century were the new intermediaries between West and East. China developed a taste for exotica from the Islamic world, which profoundly affected Chinese style in future centuries. Turkish shadow plays known as *karagoz*, musicians and musical instruments from Bukhara and Samarkand, and dancers from Tashkent were all welcome at the Tang court.

The Arabs' expansion into Asia, Africa and Europe also opened up new vistas in science and philosophy, as they began to plumb the ocean of knowledge contained in Greek manuscripts and to translate them into Arabic. Through their contacts with India and China they also followed new developments in mathematics, medicine and astronomy.

The Arabs now became the intermediaries in a dialogue that extended from China to Venice, and then westwards to France, Spain and Portugal. As well as passing on Greek science and philosophy to the newly developing world of the time, they propagated Indian mathematics, the new symbols of number and the decimal system that became the foundations of modern science. They also disseminated the science of chemistry, knowledge of the properties of metals and of new Chinese technologies, and above all medical information, which opened up great possibilities in the human and biological sciences. Muslim interest in astronomy led to the development of new concepts of the universe and of astronomy.

Although they only stayed two centuries, the Arabs left an indelible imprint on the region south of the Aral Sea, bestowing upon it the Muslim faith, which today – despite decades of religious repression under Communist rule – is still the region's predominant faith. They also introduced the Arabic script, which was widely used there for both writing and architectural decoration for 1,300 years.

The first independent Muslim state in Central Asia, that of the Samanids, emerged in the ninth century. Its capital was at Bukhara, which under Samanid rule become the showplace of Central Asia, and thanks to its strategic position astride the Silk Roads became one of great commercial and cultural centres of the Muslim world. The Samanid state stretched from Herat in Afghanistan to Isfahan in Iran; the court languages were Arabic, Persian and Turkish; and at a time when manuscripts were 'published' only by tedious hand copying, it had several privately-owned libraries that were open to the public.

Although all trace of these libraries is now obliterated, one outstanding relic of the Samanid reign remains: the dynasty's tenth-century tomb of decorative brickwork. Small and strikingly simple – a cubic building with inset corner columns supporting a squat dome – the mausoleum is regarded as one of the finest examples of early medieval architecture. By laying the mud bricks with which it was built at different angles, tenth-century craftspeople covered the building with intricate geometric patterns, and established architectural conventions – including that of a dome set on a wedge-shaped drum – which were followed in Central Asia for five centuries.

Buried for hundreds of years, the tomb of the Samanids was rediscovered in 1930 during the landscaping of the public park in which it now stands, and was restored using bricks made of clay bound with egg yolk and camels' milk, to match the originals.

Eleven caravan trails crossed at Bukhara. Bazaars were located near the gates that served these routes, and near places of worship where people always gathered. Today domed

Next spread
The Registan at Samarkand, Central Asia's noblest square flanked on three sides by the tiled facades of medieval colleges.

27

bazaars still buzz near Bukhara's ancient religious monuments, and a colourful open market bustles near the one remaining gate set in the crumbling wall, 12 kilometres (7.4 miles) long and 10 metres (32 feet) high, that once ringed the city. Gaily coloured fabrics are its most popular item, but its 'silks' are factory-made synthetics, and its carpets are also factory made.

In the shadow of Bukhara's ancient monuments, white-bearded men in traditional turbans and striped robes still gather by tree-shaded pools to drink strong black tea with their friends. Bukhara's twelfth-century Kalyan Tower soars to a height of 45 metres (148 feet) over the tiled domes and cascading cupolas of the city's mosques and bazaars. It is built of honey-coloured bricks laid in protruding and receding patterns to produce a texture like that of an elaborately knitted sweater. From the arched openings at its summit, muezzins called the faithful to prayer, sentries kept watch for the enemy during war, and condemned criminals were hurled to their deaths below.

The Kalyan Tower was built by the Karakhanid (Black Khan) Turks. As they fanned out across the steppes, tribal divisions among the Turks became more pronounced; by the eighth century such groups as the Kyrgyz and Uighurs had their own kingdoms. The principal Turkic states created during this period in Central Asia were those of the Karakhanids, the Khorezmshahs and the Seljuks.

Although they stubbornly preserved many strong traditions of their pre-Islamic past, most of the Turkic peoples embraced Islam during the eleventh and twelfth centuries. Indeed, the Turks of Central Asia replaced the Arabs as the faith's main cutting edge. Under the banner of Islam, the Seljuks swept west into Asia Minor, which makes up most of today's Turkey. In 1453 their successors, the Ottomans, conquered Constantinople, finally extinguishing Islam's old adversary, Byzantium, and carried Islam into the Balkans.

Meanwhile, successive waves of other Central Asian Turks poured southeast through the Khyber Pass and across the Indus and Ganges plains, making Islam the dominant religion of Pakistan and northern India. The first of these Turkic invaders were the Ghaznavids who, in 1008, defeated a confederacy of Hindu rulers at Peshawar, annexed the Punjab, and extended Muslim influence as far south as Lahore. Then came the Ghurid conquests, which, by the end of the eleventh century had expanded Muslim rule over most of northern India, adding Delhi and Ajmer to the Islamic realm in 1192, and two years later Bihar and Bengal. In 1206 Qutb al-Din Aybak became the first Sultan of Delhi, founding an Islamic state which gradually brought the greater part of the south Asian subcontinent under its sway, and making the city one of the jewels of Islam.

Early in the twelfth century the Mongols laid siege to Bukhara and Samarkand, and became the new rulers of Central Asia. The Mongols' conquests were of a scope and range never equalled, and had a tremendous impact on world history. The political organization of Asia and a large part of Europe was altered, and whole peoples were uprooted and dispersed, permanently changing the ethnic character of many regions. Ethnically the most striking result of the Mongol conquest was the wide dispersal of the Turkic peoples over Western Asia. Since the Mongols were not a numerous race, Genghis Khan augmented his armies with men from Turkish tribes on whose fidelity he could rely, until Turks in the Mongol armies actually outnumbered the native Mongols.

Advancing across Asia with the Mongol armies, the Tatar Turks occupied the Crimea, Kazakhs settled in the vast steppelands south of Siberia, Uzbek Turks occupied the semi-desert and oasis system on the southern rim of Central Asia, while the Turkmen roamed

THE TENTH-CENTURY DECORATIVE BRICKWORK TOMB OF THE SAMANID DYNASTY, AT BUKHARA, IS REGARDED AS ONE OF THE FINEST EXAMPLES OF EARLY MEDIEVAL ARCHITECTURE.

the deserts east of the Caspian Sea and the Azeries settled on its western shores. By the Middle Ages, Turks were sufficiently dominant in Central Asia to lend it the name Turkestan. Turkic peoples, in fact, are now one of the most widespread ethnic groups in the world – inhabiting a vast region from the Great Wall of China in the east to the Balkans in the west, and from Siberia in the north to Afghanistan in the south.

No one culture ever dominated the Silk Road. Only during the thirteenth-century Mongol empire, which included China, Central Asia, much of the Middle East and eastern Europe, was the Silk Road under the control of a single ruler. Genghis Khan and his successors ruled the massive empire by force, but also with considerable skill. Their diligent patronage of trade encouraged merchants, pilgrims and travellers, and it was during this period that European merchants were able, under Mongol protection, to safely traverse the normally unruly steppes, establishing direct contact between China and the West for the very first time.

Six centuries of sun, wind and rain have failed to dull the lustre of the ceramic tiles adorning the royal tombs of the Timurid dynasty at Shah-i-Zinda at Samarkand.

The united Mongol Empire was short-lived, but the dream of Asian empire was not dead. Declaring that the world was worth only one king, Timur set out to conquer it all. Timur, the son of a Turco-Mongol chieftain, was born in 1336. A wound in the leg, inflicted in a local rebellion, gave him the name Timur the Lame. In the West he was known as Tamerlane. He was a born leader with a genius for strategy, and an outstanding chess player. In a succession of military campaigns (fifteen campaigns in twenty-three countries) lasting half a century, Timur carved out an empire stretching from the Indus River to the Black Sea.

By 1370, the crippled warrior was undisputed leader of the steppe, and in 1380 he defeated the Il-Khans to become master of Persia. In 1398 Timur stormed through the Khyber Pass, devastated Sind and Punjab and sacked Delhi. In 1399 he invaded Georgia. In 1401 he stormed Baghdad and Damascus, and in 1402 he defeated the Turkish Ottomans in Ankara. Had he not died of pneumonia in 1405 as he was leading his armies against China, Timur might even have conquered that too.

Ordinarily his taste for battle kept the crippled monarch on the move, but between campaigns he focused his considerable energies on making Samarkand a capital worthy of his conquests. From conquered territories in Persia, India and the Middle East, Timur plundered both talented craftspeople and treasures to enhance his capital. What they created was neither Persian, Indian or Arab, although it reflected the influence of all three. Nor was it modelled on the old Samarkand. Instead, these captured architects built a city possessing a new and dazzling Tatar concept. New buildings rose out of the desert, built of mudbrick and faced with ceramic tiles in every imaginable shade of blue.

Returning to Samarkand with the loot of his Indian conquests, Timur built Central Asia's most magnificent mosque, using ninety-five captured Indian elephants to drag materials into place. The enormous star-spangled portal and colossal blue dome of Timur's tile-covered mosque – named after his favourite wife, Bibi Khanum – prompted one chronicler to write, 'Its dome would have been unique had it not been for the heavens, and unique would have been its portal had it not been for the Milky Way.' And although time and history have been merciless – an avaricious Uzbek amir melted down its metal gates to make coins, and a Russian cannon shell shattered its enamelled dome – the mosque's gauntly beautiful ruins still dominate Samarkand's skyline, and are slowly being restored. In the royal cemetery of Shah-i-Zinda, a sea of blues from darkest mauve to palest opalescent are still held in an incredibly thin glaze, undimmed by six centuries of sun, wind and rain.

Timur's descendants transformed the already spectacular city of Samarkand into one of the cultural and intellectual wonders of the Islamic world. Its observatory, colleges and mosques became intellectual gathering places for astronomers, poets, theologians and architects. Ulugh Beg, the astronomer, was Timur's grandson. The map of the heavens he drew was used as the basis for a later Gregorian star chart, and was also adopted by Chinese astrologers.

The royal astronomer also built and lectured at the first of a trio of great religious colleges which today command three of the four sides of the Registan – considered to be architecturally Central Asia's noblest square. The tiled facade of Ulugh Beg's Madrasa is decorated with enormous star patterns. Opposite, and clearly built to harmonize, is the Shirdar, or 'lion-bearing' Madrasa, so called because of the tiger in the rays of the rising sun that decorates its portal. On the north side of the square is the Tilakar, or 'gilded' Madrasa, named after the large quantities of gold used in its decoration. The south side of the magnificently restored Registan is open to the wind.

Timur's hard-won empire lasted only a few generations. His descendants quarrelled bitterly among themselves and were unable to hold together the vast steppe domain he had created. When Timur's empire disintegrated, the region fell easy prey to the Uzbeks – Turkic nomads descended from the Muslim wing of the Golden Horde. Under Uzbek rule, Bukhara boasted a different mosque in which to pray for each day of the year. With over 30,000 religious students, it had the atmosphere of a great university city, with few equals in the world at that time.

THE KALYAN TOWER
AND CASCADING
CUPOLAS OF BUKHARA'S
BAZAARS, WHERE
UZBEK WOMEN STILL
PROUDLY WEAR THEIR
TRADITIONAL RAINBOW
SILKS IN PUBLIC.

Today, Samarkand and Bukhara are no longer centres of political power. The Uzbeks' modern capital is Tashkent; the largest city in Central Asia, it has more than 2 million people and the region's only subway. According to al-Biruni, an eleventh-century Arab scholar and scientist, this city was none other than the so-called Stone Tower, where the Roman geographer Ptolemy said Western and Chinese merchants met regularly in the first century to exchange goods, but at least three other Central Asia locations have been identified as the Stone Tower. And since Tashkent was rebuilt as a showpiece of modern Soviet architecture, after a 1966 earthquake levelled a third of the city, there is little left to prove al-Biruni's claim. Monolithic buildings squat in vast squares, and where caravan trails once crossed there is today an enormous divided-highway intersection dominated by a twenty-three-storey hotel.

Central Asia suffered severe economic decline following the demise of overland East–West trade, and split into three warring khanates of Khiva, Bukhara and Kokand. Divided and disorganized, the region was no longer capable of playing an important role in history or even of maintaining its independence. In the nineteenth century the Russians began to advance into Central Asia. By 1900, they had conquered it all. Finally in 1927 the Soviets – successors of the Russian empire after the communist revolution of 1917 – divided Central Asia into six republics, naming them after the region's major Turkic nationalities: Azerbaijan, Kazakstan, Kyrgyzstan, Turkmenistan and Uzbekistan, plus Persian-speaking Tajikstan. China could not prevent what it called Outer Mongolia from falling under Soviet control as well, but it retained its rule over eastern Turkestan, which it turned into a province, then after China's own communist revolution into the Xinjiang Uighur autonomous region.

As repressive as it was, Soviet rule did introduce the basics of science and technology, established schools and universities, and laid the foundations of a modern industrial society – along with pollution and environmental damage. It was a flawed but vital legacy on which to build.

Soviet cultural policy in Central Asia was to make painstaking reconstructions of important buildings or entire complexes. Buildings were well looked after, and preserved for posterity under Soviet rule, but a growing number of critics maintained it would be best to be less ambitious, and instead to preserve them as they stood. The choice seems to be between arrested decay, a noble ruin, or a dead imitation of the real thing.

No ruin is nobler than that of Timur's White Palace at his birthplace of Shakhrisabz (Kesh), near the Afghan border. All that remains are two giant fragments of what was the largest human-made arch of its time: 50 metres (165 feet) high, with a 22-metre (74 feet) span. Even in decay, the tiles adorning the ruined palace portal are magnificent. Their lustre has outlived the empires of Timurids, the Uzbeks and the Czars, and it has now managed to outlive communism too.

Timur, once vilified by the communists as a ruthless tyrant, is a national hero again; a statue of the warrior on horseback has replaced Marx in a central square of Tashkent. The mausoleum where he is buried – beneath a massive monolith of dark green jade, below a dome gilded with three kilograms (96 troy ounces) of gold – has been lavishly restored. Today, references to Timur in the Tashkent newspapers have to be politically correct. He is referred to as Amir Timur – Lord Timur; the historical epithet Timur-I-Leng (Timur the Lame) is now not allowed. That he was lame and famously ugly is rarely mentioned.

Independence caught the Turkic republics by surprise, and has left them with many problems. All are new entities and unfamiliar with democracy; all are in the process of building new political and economic systems; and all rely heavily on former Communist Party officials to run their countries. Since the abortive 1991 coup in Moscow caused communism to implode, Marxist ideology has been replaced with a more populist, nationalist creed. Moreover, each republic is different.

Also, since 80 per cent of their trade had been with the former USSR, the dislocations of independence have been costly. But despite their struggling economies, the Turkic republics of Eurasia hold more than enough natural riches to transform their people's lives. In Uzbekistan, the largest gold mine on earth produces 50 tons of ore a year. Kazakstan and Azerbaijan have oilfields rivalling the Middle East's, while Turkmenistan ranks fourth among all nations in reserves of natural gas.

The break-up of the former Soviet Union triggered a scramble for influence over the new nations of Central Asia. In an echo of the 'Great Game' played by European imperial powers as they vied for influence over the region at the end of the nineteenth century, others are now competing for a hold.

Although today they have little economic importance in the patterns of world trade, transportation routes across Central Asia have reopened. Convoys of Iranian trucks head north for Russia, and Turkish trucks drive east to Kyrgyzstan. Railway links have opened between Iran and Turkmenistan in the west, and between China and Kazakstan in the east. And adventurous travelers are rediscovering the faded glories of the Silk Road.

RICH PASTURES OF UZBEKISTAN'S FERGHANA VALLEY, HOME TO A BREED OF SO-CALLED, CELESTIAL HORSES. CHINA'S QUEST FOR THESE HORSES LED TO ITS FIRST CONTACTS WITH THE WEST.

TURKMEN GIRLS PLAYING TRADITIONAL MOUTH HARP.

© TOBY MOLENAAR

THE MOUNTAIN PASSAGE

'The Roof of the World' is the name given to the apex of some of the Earth's mightiest mountain ranges: the Pamir, Tian Shan, Karakoram, Himalaya and Hindu Kush. A natural barrier between China and the West, these ranges were – and still are – one of the biggest obstacles for Silk Road travellers.

REMOTE BORDERLANDS BETWEEN CHINA AND CENTRAL ASIA. ZHANG QIAN, CONSIDERED AS THE FATHER OF THE SILK ROAD, JOURNEYED THROUGH THESE IN THE SECOND CENTURY B.C.

SUCH WAS THE STATUS OF FERGHANA HORSES FROM CENTRAL ASIA THAT CERAMIC MODELS WERE OFTEN INTERRED WITH THEIR WEALTHY CHINESE OWNERS.

Through these remote high regions, in the second century B.C., journeyed the so-called 'father' of the Silk Road, Zhang Qian. He was sent by the Han emperor Wu to seek alliances among the peoples of Central Asia against China's chief enemy, the Huns. Historians consider it one of the most important journeys of antiquity. Although he failed in his mission – he was twice captured by the Huns, failed to forge any alliances and returned after thirteen years with only one of his original 100 men – the wandering of the indefatigable Zhang Qian laid the groundwork for the Silk Road.

Zhang Qian traveled as far as Afghanistan, and took back to China knowledge of many distant lands like Persia, Syria and a place known as Li-jien – thought to have been Rome. This knowledge increased China's awareness of its western neighbours, and soon led to regular contacts with them. Emperor Wu was particularly impressed by the stories Zhang Qian brought back of a breed of 'celestial horses' raised on the rich pasture lands of Ferghana. Big, strong and intelligent, they seemed to be the perfect answer to the slashing cavalry tactics of the Huns.

When the people of Ferghana refused to part with their fine breeding stock, the Han emperor sent a 60,000-man army 4,000 kilometres (2,500 miles) across the Taklamakan Desert and the Tian Shan to capture them, opening up Central Asia to Chinese power for the first time and paving the way for China's first contacts with the West.

During the Tang dynasty, the 'heavenly horses' were immortalized by Chinese artists and sculptors. The most splendid example is the famous 'Flying horse', one hoof poised on a swallow's back, excavated by Chinese archaeologists near Xian in 1969. Although this breed is long extinct, the rearing and riding of fine horses is still an important feature of the region.

This we were to see ourselves, as hurried along by icy winds and snow flurries, we were taken by bus to a remote plain to witness one of the last vestiges of the ancient nomadic empires of the steppe: a Kazakh rodeo. There, silhouetted against the darkening sky for all the world like Genghis Khan's cavalry, were some 1,000 men, women and children, hunched on horseback or huddled in carts, awaiting the main attraction of the day – us – for foreigners are rare in this remote corner of Central Asia. There could not have been a sharper contrast: we with our soft skins and heated minibuses, and they with their creased leather faces and sturdy steppe ponies.

Our mutual curiosity satisfied, the Kazakhs, a nation descended from the Turkic and Mongol tribes of the Golden Horde, turned their attention to the skilled riding that they do best. First, fifty youngsters galloped round and round a flag-marked course in a gruelling mini-marathon; then women pursued men on horseback and beat them with their riding whips in what we were told was an ancient, and no doubt endearing, form of Kazakh courtship; and finally there was a game of *ulak tartysh*, an unruly battle-game played – or fought – over a goat's carcass. As we left, army officers there to supervise the game were wading into the melee themselves.

The valleys and passes of 'The Roof of the World' have provided lines of communication between Central Asia, China and India since ancient times. One of these was the 'Road North' through the Tian Shan range. Another crossed the Pamirs to Afghanistan, while a third linked China to India over the Karakorams.

With police cars front and rear and guards posted at key points en route, we first followed the 'Road North' in a convoy of seven red and white buses across the then Sino-Soviet border zone. The mosque at Panfilov, the last town on the Soviet side of the frontier, spoke volumes: the facade was typical of the austere Islamic architecture of Central Asia, while the minaret was shaped like an ornate Chinese pagoda.

Politics, however, do not mix as easily as cultures, and for centuries differences between Russia and China ran deep in the Ili Valley – a natural corridor for trade and conquest between the two countries. In 1870 the Russians occupied the Ili region of China, and although they withdrew a decade later the area remained a bone of contention – a sensitive region almost permanently closed to foreigners, and the site of occasional flare-ups of armed conflict.

Passing through this usually closed frontier at Hurgos – shortly before Kazakstan, which now borders China, gained its independence – we went from one world to another. The Soviet side was a walled outpost, deserted except for troops and border officials, efficient but aloof. The Chinese side, in contrast, was chaotic and friendly. It opened up directly into the town, where soldiers played drums and cymbals, lion dancers pranced in the streets and hundreds of people turned out to greet us. En route by bus to our hotel in Yining, a town normally off-limits to foreigners, our 'guide' made up for his total lack of English by serenading us in Chinese.

We were now in the Xinjiang Uighur autonomous region, formerly Chinese Turkestan. A vast 1,650,000 square kilometre (637,000 square mile) area of steppe, desert and mountain, it covers one-sixth of China's total land area and is its largest administrative unit. Here, the people are mainly Turkic and Muslim, and despite Chinese efforts to resettle the region it retains a distinct Central Asian atmosphere of its own.

Although the 'Road North' crosses the Heavenly Mountains at their relatively low-lying eastern extremity, we were soon in trouble. Picture-card scenes of towering Tian Shan pines in steep-sided valleys were obliterated by driving snow. Our minibuses, lacking snow chains, began slithering all over the road. Finally we came to a dead stop on an icy incline littered with stranded trucks.

Advance seemed impossible, retreat unthinkable. But we had reckoned without that unique Chinese substitute for machines – the people power that has been crucial to the development of modern China. The officials, soldiers and guides accompanying us simply dragged the buses up the mountain without most of the passengers even having to get off.

Once over the mountains the snow stopped and we picnicked by a frozen lake: it was too cold to stay still but the views were spectacular. For the rest of the day we drove across endless seemingly unpopulated plateaus, followed by the ever-present peaks of the Tian Shan. Fourteen bone-shaking hours later, with our guide singing lustily to keep our driver awake, we arrived in Shihezi.

The worst, however, was over. The next day dawned bright and sunny, and it was but a brief further bus ride to the railroad station and – to our vast relief – a 'soft class' train, the Chinese equivalent of first class. Ours was the first passenger train to travel on the newly laid track between Shihezi and Urumqi, and we were given a rousing send-off: banners in English and Chinese fluttered over the newly built platform as children with classically made-up faces sang us farewell.

Being winched over the river that forms the border with Tajikstan was an unorthodox way to enter Afghanistan on the second of our three journeys across the Roof of the World. But then little about Afghanistan was normal: over two decades of conflict and three years of drought had left increased poverty, as well as death and destruction throughout the land. And although fighting and famine had subsided, the humanitarian crisis was far from over, and the task of rebuilding the devastated nation had hardly begun.

Out of a total population of 23 million, the United Nations (UN) estimates that 1.5 million Afghans died, 2 million were wounded and 5 million more made refugees in fighting that started with the Soviet invasion in 1979 and ended in 2001 with the toppling by US-led forces of the Taliban. Meanwhile severe drought from 1999 to 2001 devastated Afghanistan's agriculture and decimated its herds, on which the livelihood of 85 per cent of the population depends.

Travelling with Muslim aid workers through the Pamirs, across the northern Afghan plains and over the Hindu Kush to Kabul, we saw many villages abandoned, and towns and cities badly damaged with only intermittent running water and electricity. Parts of Kabul lay buried beneath thousands of tons of rubble. In the countryside roamed armed men who needed to be lured to give up their guns with jobs and aid.

More than a year after the fall of the Taliban, however, little had arrived of the US$4.5 billion pledged by wealthy nations to rebuild Afghanistan, and most of what had arrived had been spent on emergency relief rather than reconstruction. The Aga Khan Development Network (AKDN) engineers, who winched us across the upper reaches of the Amu Darya (ancient Oxus) river into Afghanistan, were engaged in the only major construction project we witnessed. They were building bridges to connect the northeastern Afghan province of Badakhshan with its Central Asian neighbours.

Crossing the remote highlands of Badakhshan, the war debris-littered passes of the Hindu Kush, and the impoverished Afghan plains, it was difficult to imagine this devastated land as it once was: a centre of empires, a birthplace of art styles and an international crossroads of culture and commerce.

An early urban Bronze Age civilization that arose in northern Afghanistan developed an active caravan trade linking the civilizations of the Indus Valley and Mesopotamia. By this route the finest lapis lazuli in the world was brought west from the highlands of Badakhshan to Sumer and Egypt 5,000 years ago. Later, Afghanistan was joined to India by a 4,200 kilometre (2,600 mile) road built by Indian's Maurya dynasty, and was linked to Central Asia and the Middle East by the imperial highways of the Persians.

Traces of intense cultural activity once marked these routes that centuries ago joined east and west, north and south across Afghanistan. Ruins of ancient cities, such as Kapisa in the heart of Afghanistan, and Ai Khanoum and Tillia Tepe on the northern Afghan plains, told a story of complex exchanges with other lands. At Ai Khanoum, archaeologists discovered an orientalized Greek city; at Kapisa they unearthed a treasure trove of Indian ivories, Chinese lacquers and Roman art, and at Tillia Tepe they found

ONCE ONE OF THE PROUDEST MONUMENTS OF THE SILK ROAD, THIS GIANT BUDDHA IN THE BAMIYAN VALLEY, IN AFGHANISTAN, WAS REDUCED TO RUBBLE BY TALIBAN ARTILLERY IN MARCH 2001.

motifs reflecting the disparate artistic styles of India, Greece, Iran, China and the nomads of Central Asia.

After Alexander the Great invaded the region in the fourth century B.C., his successors created wealthy kingdoms in Afghanistan that bridged the civilizations of East and West, notably giving rise to Gandharan art, which beautifully blended Greek stonecarving skills with Buddhist themes. In the early centuries of our era Afghanistan was the centre of the vast Kushan empire which acted as an intermediary in trade between India, China and Rome. In the fifteenth century Herat, in northwestern Afghanistan, was capital of the Timurid Empire and one of Asia's most verdant centres of art and learning.

War, systematic theft and illegal excavations have devastated much of Afghanistan's rich and varied heritage, which vividly illustrated several high points in the history of civilization over the past 2,500 years. Kabul Museum was looted, and many archaeological sites were dug up and sold abroad. Finally, the decree of Taliban spiritual leader Mullah Omar on 26 February 2001, ordering 'all non-Islamic statues and tombs' to be destroyed, led to the much-publicized demolition of the monumental Buddhas of Bamiyan.

The valley of Bamiyan lies at the heart of the Hindu Kush mountains about 150 miles northwest of Kabul. During the early centuries of our era endless caravans of luxury-laden camels, plodding along the Silk Road, passed through the valley. Later Buddhist monks joined these caravans, and a great religious centre burgeoned in Bamiyan. About A.D. 400 the pilgrim Fa-Hsien came to Bamiyan from China and described a sumptuous assembly attended by such large numbers of monks that they came, it seemed, 'as if in clouds'. Two hundred years later another Chinese pilgrim, Hsuan-tsang, reported more than ten monasteries with over 1,000 monks.

The great wonders at Bamiyan were two of the world's largest Buddhas, carved into the face of the sandstone cliff dominating the town from the north. To the east of the cliff, probably the oldest of these two statues stood 38 metres (125 feet) tall. The other, to the west of the cliff, measured 55 metres (180 feet). Around and between them a maze of cells and sanctuaries were painstakingly cut out, and those around the statues were interconnected to allow worshippers to perform the rite of circumambulation. The ceilings and walls were smoothed over with mud-and-straw plaster and then painted with inspirational scenes. The Buddhas were probably created during the third to fourth centuries; the murals mainly during the seventh.

Today, all that remains of the two giant Buddhas are forlorn piles of rubble at the bottom of the enormous, now eerily empty niches in which they once stood. Caves in the cliff face that once served as cells for Buddhist monks are now home for homeless Hazara families. At the base of the cliff what was once a thriving bazaar lies devastated by civil war.

At an altitude of 3,363 metres (11,000 feet) we drove through the Salang Tunnel, linking northern Afghanistan with the valleys of Koh Daman and Kabul. After years of neglect, the tunnel was in a dangerous state of disrepair, with water cascading down its walls and lumps of concrete hanging from its ceiling. We covered its 2.7-kilometre (1.7 mile)-long fume-filled interior as quickly as the poor visibility and huge potholes would permit.

Emerging from the Hindu Kush mountains we crossed the Begram Plain which, because of its strategic location at the southern base of the Hindu Kush, has in recent years been a virtual war zone. It guards passes through mountain ranges fanning out from the towering Hindu Kush across the centre of the country. In ancient times these passes were gateways to India, China and Central Asia, and Alexander the Great built a city here, which the Kushans later made capital of their vast empire. They called it Kapisa.

The Begram Plain is desolate today, but in 1939 French archaeologists excavating the

ruins of Kapisa discovered a treasure trove testifying to the existence here, nearly 2,000 years ago, of a highly refined and cultured citizenry. The extent of international trade at this period is best exemplified by the discovery of the so-called Begram Treasure. Hidden in a chamber of the royal city, it comprised painted glassware from Alexandria in Egypt, Chinese lacquered furniture encrusted with Indian ivory, and a bronze statuette of a deity from an eastern province of the Roman empire.

Approaching Kabul via the Koh Daman Valley we passed hundreds of abandoned villages, thousands of destroyed homes and millions of withered vines. Crippled tanks, burnt-out trucks and twisted artillery pieces littered the roadside, which was lined by signs warning of landmines. Koh Daman was once one of the richest and most beautiful valleys in the country. It was noted mainly for its vineyards, but almond, pear, apricot, fig and cherry trees also once flourished here. Not any more, for this was the line of attack on Kabul or – depending on which way the war was going – retreat to the fastness of the Hindu Kush. Today most of the Koh Daman Valley vines are dead and its orchards destroyed, their fruit trees stripped for firewood.

Entering Kabul along roads littered with more debris of war, we passed the remains of what was the first Moghul 'Paradise Garden' and the predecessor of many other famous imperial gardens in the South Asian subcontinent. Built by Babur, the founder of the Moghul Empire, Bagh-e-Babur was once covered by magnificent stands of chinar trees, wild rose and jasmine, but – like much else in Kabul – it now lies in ruins.

Babur, who claimed direct descent from both Genghis Khan and Timur (Tamerlane), seized Kabul and carved out a kingdom in Afghanistan, from where in 1525 he launched his invasion of India to become the first of the Moghul emperors. Babur never forgot Kabul, however, and when he died in 1539 he was buried there, according to his wishes, in Bagh-e-Babur.

Babur invaded India through the Khyber Pass, Central Asia's main gateway to the subcontinent. A young soldier with an ageing rifle, who fortunately was not called upon to protect us from the Kalashnikov-carrying Pathans of the semi-autonomous Tribal Areas of northwest Pakistan, escorted us through the Khyber Pass, which in places narrows to as little as 16 metres (52 feet).

From the headquarters of the colourful Khyber Rifles, near the head of the pass, the road first snakes through craggy canyons beneath armour-plated watch towers manned by Pakistan's Frontier Force. It then descends in wide sweeps, past fortified Pathan compounds with high mudbrick walls, menacing gun turrets and massive iron gates, to the Punjab Plain below. Metre for metre, this is possibly the world's most heavily fortified stretch of road.

A sign near the foot of the Khyber Pass proclaims, 'Everybody who was ever anybody passed this way'. Among the 'anybodies' was Rudyard Kipling, who wrote, 'The snowbound trade of the north comes down, to the market square of Peshawar town.' It still does. When we arrived, however, Peshawar's market square, Chowk Yadgar, was being torn up to build an underground car park. Peshawar's bazaars remain though, among the most exotic in Asia. Here, from shoebox-sized shops, carts and stalls squeezed into a maze of alleys, all manner of merchandise is bought and sold – from

THE KHYBER PASS, FOR CENTURIES CENTRAL ASIA'S MAIN GATEWAY TO INDIA FOR TRADE AND CONQUEST. TODAY, IT IS DEFENDED BY THE LEGENDARY KHYBER RIFLES (LEFT).

elaborately constructed bouquets of bank notes for newly-weds to bullet-studded bandoliers, as well as a whole range of colourful tribal garments, silks, copperware, carpets and jewellery.

Now, as always, Peshawar is very much a frontier town, where turbaned Punjabi farmers from the plains rub shoulders with Pathans from the hills in rolled felt caps. An ancient and atmospheric town of bazaars and caravanserais, Peshawar is a tribal trading post and home of the exotic Qissa Khawani Bazaar, immortalized by Kipling as the 'Street of Storytellers'. Once a principal stopping place for caravans carrying goods – and fantastic stories – from far off lands, Peshawar, at the foot of the Khyber Pass, has survived dozens of invasions. The Bala Hissar Fortress, built in 1519 by the Moghul Emperor Babur, still dominates the city centre. The fierce, bearded Pathans, tribesmen who inhabit Peshawar and the rest of Pakistan's northwest frontier province, successfully drove off the British, the Mongols, the Persians and Greeks.

PESHAWAR'S BAZAARS ARE STILL AMONG THE MOST EXOTIC IN ASIA.

Alexander the Great's lightning attack on India, his return march through the desert to Susa and his sudden death in Babylon are the stuff of legend, and have never been forgotten. The Sultans of Delhi, the first Muslim rulers of northern India, adopted for themselves in the thirteenth century the title *Sikander al-sani* – the second Alexander – symbolizing their role as conquerors of India. Even in the twentieth century in the Kafiristan and Hunza regions of north Pakistan, he is claimed as ancestor by fair-skinned and fair-haired inhabitants.

Although Greek rule in these regions survived less than twenty-five years, Greek culture was more permanent. Alexander's conquests took place at a time when Greek art and thought were in fullest flower, and the peoples of Asia were quick to adopt – and adapt – its aesthetics. The most striking result was a hybrid art form combining Western Classical stone carving skills with Indian Buddhist themes, which takes its name from the region where it flourished: Gandhara, comprising roughly the Kabul Valley of southeast Afghanistan and northwest Pakistan.

Shortly after Alexander invaded Central Asia, Chandragupta Maurya seized the throne of the Indian kingdom of Magadha, thus taking the first step in the creation of the mighty Mauryan empire. The rulers of the Mauryan Empire, which stretched from the Indus to Brahmaputra and from the Himalayas to the Vindhya range, recognized that the unity of a great empire depended on the quality of its roads. A 'Ministry of Public Works' was responsible for construction and maintenance of the roads and rest houses, and for the smooth running of the many ferries that carried these Royal Roads across the wide rivers.

Central Asia was joined to India by a 4,200 kilometre (2,600 mile) road that passed through the Khyber Pass and drove diagonally across the subcontinent to the Bay of Bengal, following the course of the River Ganges. It was this road – now renamed the Great Trunk Road – that we took from Peshawar to Taxila, where more than six ancient cities were built one on top of the other. It was established in 600 B.C., later ruled by Alexander the Great, and then by the Buddhist Kushan Empire.

The historical Buddha was born in approximately 563 B.C. in Lumbini, a village in what is now southern Nepal, close to the Indian border. The son of a warrior-caste prince, he was given the personal name Siddhartha. Prince Siddhartha left his father's kingdom as a young man and lived his adult life in the northeast Indian state of Magadha, now called Bihar, where he founded the Buddhist religion. After his death in 483 B.C., at the age of 80, in the Indian town now known as Kushinagar, Buddhism spread over vast distances throughout and beyond India, and rapidly became the faith of more than a third of Asia's population.

It was at the time of the second century A.D. during the reign of Kushan King Kanishka I that the religion of the Buddha spread from Gandhara in northwest India through Bactria – roughly today's Afghanistan – to Central Asia and China. Kanishka was a great patron of Gandharan art, and under his rule international trade also flourished: artefacts unearthed at the Kushan capital of Begram included the Begram Treasure mentioned above.

Traffic on the Great Trunk Road is suicidal, but the trucks and buses that bore down on us three abreast were at least colourful: covered from bumper to bumper with paintings of Muslim shrines, landscapes and wildlife, intricate patterns and portraits of film stars from East and West.

Leaving the Great Trunk Road and its unique traffic art, we joined yet another great highway: the Karakoram, linking Islamabad, the capital of Pakistan, with the fabled trading city of Kashgar in Chinese Turkestan. Carved through the Karakoram and Himalayan ranges, the highway is an epic feat of modern-day engineering. It winds its way up to a height of 4,877 metres (16,000 feet) past sheer rock walls, below glaciers and over icy mountain passes, among eight of the ten highest peaks in the world, including K2, the world's second-highest mountain. The 15,000 Pakistani and 10,000 Chinese workers employed on the construction of the road endured the extreme heat of the Indus Valley and the bitter cold of the mountain passes, and for almost every kilometre built one of them lost their lives.

The 805 kilometre (500 mile) metalled road first leads around the westernmost part of the Himalayan range and the tremendous massif of the Nanga Parbat, which at 8,126 metres (26,660 feet) is the eighth highest mountain in the world and western anchor of the Himalayan range. It then follows first the Indus, then Gilgit and finally the Hunza River valleys through the Karakoram range to the Khunjerab Pass, where at a height of 4,697 metres it reaches the Chinese border. There it crosses the autonomous Tajik county of northwest China and descends to the balmy oasis of Kashgar. It took us a week's hard driving to make this journey.

For its sheer mountain grandeur and breathtaking panorama of beauty, few places can match the superb landscape through which the Karakoram Highway snakes. The average Karakoram peak is above 6,100 metres (20,000 feet), double that of the Alps or Rockies.

The Karakoram Highway follows the old pilgrimage route from China to the Buddhist land of Gandhara. About 3,000 inscriptions and more than 2,000 petroglyphs were discovered along it. Rocky outcroppings abound with images of horned animals, hunters, and Buddhist *stupas*. A hundred and twenty-five travellers have immortalized themselves by scratching their names on a single rock. The rocks, which were initially polished by water and debris, were in the course of the millennia coated in a patina of brown and blue hues, called 'desert varnish'. Artists of prehistoric times discovered the possibility of making pictures visible from a long distance by taking off small parts of the rock surface, by pecking with a point stone.

Gilgit is Pakistan's major terminus for trade with China. The mixture of goods in its open-fronted shops gives it a distinct flavour – Mongolian scarves, copying machines, Chinese porcelain, Japanese motorbikes, and an array of locally embroidered woollen scarves, vests, and greatcoats hand-woven by local craftspeople, along with apricot-oil lamps, muzzle-loading muskets, snowshoes, thick blankets and embroidered skull caps.

ALTIT FORT (ABOVE), WHICH ONCE COMMANDED PASSAGE ALONG THE SILK ROAD, TODAY STANDS DERELICT. TRADE NOW FLOWS UNHINDERED ALONG THE INDUS VALLEY (ABOVE RIGHT) TO GILGIT (BELOW RIGHT), PAKISTAN'S MAIN STAGING POST FOR TRADE WITH CHINA.

Gilgit is an ancient tribal town situated in a green, irrigated oasis at the southern reaches of the Mintaka Pass. It is famous as the home of the world's highest polo grounds and for inventing a rough and tumble freestyle version of the game that was later taken to the West by the British, who also played their own 'great game' – espionage – with the Russians in these mountains.

A four-hour drive from Gilgit, passing under the north face of Rakaposhi – a fantastic 7,778 metre (25,550 feet) precipice of snow and ice – is Hunza, a lovely valley located amid glaciers and sub-polar ice fields. Its people are famous for robust health and a longevity said to often exceed 100 years. Notorious brigands who once preyed on Silk Road caravans, the origin of the Hunzakuts is a mystery. They are not ethnically related to any of their neighbours, and their language, Burushaski, is one of only two in the world – the other being Basque – that is unrelated to any other known tongue. Their Aryan appearance and light colouring, blue eyes and brown hair are attributed by some to Greek soldiers from Alexander the Great's conquering army who settled here at the time of his campaigns.

Hunzakuts are Ismaili Muslims, followers of Imam Karim Aga Khan, in whose honour the name of Hunza's capital was recently changed from Baltit to Karimabad. The 2,682 metre (8,800 feet) town sits high on a rocky perch, surrounded by terraced hillsides framed by poplars, wheat fields and orchards of apricot, apples, walnuts and mulberries. The fairytale-like Baltit Fort, which was built about 600 years ago, looks over the valley, and Ultar Glacier hangs broodingly above it all. Originally Baltit Fort was both residence and redoubt of the Mirs – an admixture of ruler, king, religious leader and landlord – of Hunza. Baltit Fort was recently restored by the Aga Khan Trust for Culture.

Hunzakuts have a reputation of living to their ripe old age by following a regime of apricots, yoghurt, nuts and 'Hunza water', the local colourless firewater made from mulberries of an indescribable flavour reminiscent of wood. Because of their simple diet and constant exercise – before the highway was constructed they would think nothing of walking 104 kilometres (65 miles) to Gilgit to make purchases in the bazaar – they are known as one of the world's healthiest people. Their isolation ended with construction of Karakoram Highway. White bread, sugar and Coca-Cola – along with tourism – have crept in.

The Karakoram range is both boundary and barrier between China and Pakistan, and the 4,880 metre (16,000 feet) high, 136 kilometre (85 mile) long Khunjerab Pass is the gateway through it. At its summit, bored Pakistani and Chinese border guards huddle in shelters a quarter of a mile apart. Walking – slowly, because of the high altitude – we crossed between them.

Tashkurghan, a small town dominated by a ruined fortress, sits on a windswept plateau two hours' drive into China. The name means 'stone tower', and this was known to ancient Silk Road travellers as the place where traders from the East and West bartered goods. It is now the center of the Tajik autonomous county of China's westernmost region, Xinjiang.

Like their cousins living across the border in Tajikstan, the 26,000 Tajiks living in the extreme west of China speak the Tajik language, which is related to Persian. Tajiks have been the occupiers of High Asia since earliest times; they are skilled farmers, craftspeople and traders, whose sedentary culture was copied by many of Central Asia's nomads. Today, ironically, the Tajiks of China are mainly nomadic herders.

From Tashkurghan on the headwaters of the Yarkand River, the way lay over rocky spurs and through defiles where swollen

rivers had swept away the entire sections of the road, and but for our four-wheel-drive vehicles we would have never have got through. Finally, after passing more breathtaking mountain scenery, including the famous 7,529 metre (24,700 feet) Muztagata 'Father of Icebergs' Glacier, we slowly descended into the balmy Kashgar oasis.

Kashgar, in far western China, is surrounded on three sides by some of the highest mountains in the world, and the fourth side is blocked by desert. Here caravans rested between two of the most hazardous obstacles of the Silk Roads: the icy heights of the 'Roof of the World' and the arid wastes of the Taklamakan Desert, whose name in Turkic means 'who enters, never returns'. Here too, where the British, Russian and Chinese Empires met, was played out the 'great game', the extraordinary, centuries-long espionage war between Britain and Russia for control of Central Asia, fictionalized in Rudyard Kipling's *Kim*.

Even today, only the most determined travelers reach Kashgar. Despite its isolation and its exotic history, Kashgar is slowly being turned into a modern town, where the former British and Russian consulates, once hotbeds of espionage, now serve merely as hotels.

Once a week, however, some of Kashgar's old magic returns when thousands of people trek in on foot or in creaking donkey carts from miles around to buy, sell or simply browse at the city's Sunday market, one of the oldest and largest in Central Asia. Arriving in a steady stream from dawn onwards, they spread out their wares on the edge of town: magnificent fox furs and cast-off clothing, colourful Kirgiz carpets and battered bicycles, ornate daggers and sacks of grain.

By noon, there is hardly room to move. Men in black corduroy frock coats, knee-high leather boots and fur-trimmed hats haggle over merchandise, or take turns in a nearby clearing test-riding horses at breakneck speeds. Half a dozen two-humped Bactrian camels, patiently awaiting buyers, recall more glorious days when it was their steady, mile-eating gait that provided the main link between China and the West.

ONCE A WEEK THOUSANDS OF UIGHURS TREK IN ON FOOT OR IN DONKEY CARTS FROM MILES AROUND TO TRADE AT KASHGAR'S SUNDAY MARKET; BY NOON THERE IS HARDLY ANY ROOM TO MOVE.

THE STEPPE ROUTE

THE SWEEPING GRASSLANDS AND TOWERING MOUNTAINS OF MONGOLIA, CRADLE OF THE POWERFUL NOMADIC NATIONS WHO ROSE TO CONTROL THE SILK ROAD.

A PORTRAIT HEAD OF KUL TEGIN, MILITARY COMMANDER OF THE ALTAI TURKS.

© TOBY MOLENAAR

The Year of the Monkey was living up to its reputation for meteorological mayhem. One minute we were sunning ourselves by Lake Durgun Nuur in western Mongolia; the next we were struggling to stop our campsite being flattened by a storm. Our drivers formed their vehicles into a windbreak, and we held on grimly to our flimsy one-person tents. But to no avail: one by one they collapsed and their contents scattered across the steppe.

Life on the steppe never was easy – one reason it produced such fierce nomad warriors as Genghis Khan. For us sedentary types it was a gruelling journey across Mongolia in his footsteps. We were retracing the Steppe Route across Eurasia, along which wave after wave of horse nomads – the Scythians, Huns and Turks as well as the Mongols – swept west to conquer large parts of the known world.

It was also by this route that Chinese silk first found its way to Europe. For besides providing grass – the only essential ingredient for creation of a nomad empire – the Eurasian steppe also served for centuries as an extensive trade route. Within its bounds cross-country movement was easy for anyone with a horse to ride, and nomadic tribes migrating westward in the sixth century B.C. carried silk with them.

The Steppe Route was the merchants' favoured passage when the Mongols were masters of the normally dangerous steppes, for they imposed within their empire – which included China, southern Russia and Central Asia – a respect for law and order that was absolute. But incessant warfare and raiding by the nomad tribes who swirled around the heart of Asia kept this route closed for most of the time. No fully satisfactory explanation has ever been offered for the periodic explosion of nomadic peoples from the Eurasian steppe, but the pattern is clear. The region has historically been a sort of dynamo generating population movements that have affected Europe, the Middle East and Asia since the beginning of time.

Powerful nomadic empires rose repeatedly from the Eurasian steppe to assume dominion over the known world. The hard nomadic life developed not only herding skills, but also courage, endurance and military prowess. The nomads' dynamic leaders – Genghis Khan, Attila the Hun and Timur the Lame – are synonymous with brilliance in military strategy, while their mounted bowmen were among the most feared warriors the world has known.

Less well known, however, are the nomads' role in linking the sedentary civilizations of East and West, and their lasting contribution to world culture in general. Besides raiders and rulers, the nomads also came as traders or transport personnel. Steppe nomads devised forms of culture particularly suited to their mobile way of life, which spread throughout the world. Saddle and stirrup originated among the nomads, who made trousers a garment of daily wear. They invented various kinds of mobile dwellings – known as *gers* or *yurts* – and devised different ways of processing milk products. The history of the violin too began in the nomad world.

The Eurasian steppe is a vast belt of grassland extending some 8,000 kilometres (5,000 miles) from Hungary in the west, through the Ukraine and Central Asia, to

a people called the Juan-juan, who were driven from Mongolia by the Turks, migrated as far west as Hungary.

The Turks too eventually migrated west, leaving behind in Mongolia the first written record of steppe history and many stone statues erected in honour of their nobles. Five of these we encountered at Jargalan in the foothills of the Altai range as our convoy began its climb through the mountains dividing the Western and Eastern steppes. Although badly eroded by centuries of wind and rain, two still clearly portrayed a man's head and trunk, and gazed impassively at the snow-covered peaks of the Altais – the highest mountains in Mongolia and the Turks' original homeland.

HUHNER CAMP, AT THE FOOT OF THE ALTAI MOUNTAIN RANGE, WHICH DIVIDES THE WESTERN AND EASTERN STEPPES OF MONGOLIA.

Our destination that day was Huhner Camp, a mountain 'resort' nestled among pine trees in an Alp-like valley watered by a foaming stream. With an average altitude of 1,580 metres (4,720 feet), Mongolia is one of the highest countries in the world, and Siberian winds make the Eastern steppe chilly even in summer.

As milder temperatures and higher rainfall in the west made for far richer pastureland than in the east, nomads tended to migrate westward towards more inviting grasslands. A better pasture, however, was likely to be someone else's, and attempts to graze it often led to war. Typically, the movement of one people precipitated a whole series of other migrations. For example, in the second century B.C. the Hsiung-nu – known in the West as the Hun – expelled the Yue-chi from western China. The retreating Yue-chi pushed the Sakas into Bactria, where they destroyed the Greek kingdom established there by Alexander the Great, and the fleeing remnants of its people took refuge in India.

Some of the earliest evidence of these westward migrations are deer stones: upright stone slabs engraved with symbols of the sun, stylized pictures of running deer – with bird-like mouths, large round eyes and elegant spiral antlers – and weapons, including daggers and bows. Common features of the Mongolian landscape, deer stones were erected, singly and in groups, by Bronze and Early Iron Age inhabitants of the steppe, and were either tombstones, markings delineating tribal pastures or hunting signs. A few stones with similar deer carvings have also been found in Kazakstan, and in the Caucasus and Black Sea regions, indicating that this ancient art form – first created in Mongolia in the second millennium B.C. – was carried west by migrating nomads in the following centuries.

We first came across deer-stones at Ehbulag, en route from Huhner Camp to the former fortress town of Uliastay, which – wedged in by mountains on all sides, at an altitude of 1,750 metres (4,250 feet) – is one of the most remote provincial capitals of Mongolia. Once, however, it was the headquarters of the commander-in-chief of Chinese forces, who under the Manchu (Qing) dynasty occupied Mongolia from the eighteenth to the beginning of the twentieth century.

After the fall of the Manchu dynasty in 1912, Mongol princes supported by Czarist Russia declared Mongolia's independence from China. When the Czarist regime fell in 1917, Mongolia reverted to Chinese control, but with the help of Red Army troops the Mongolians defeated the Chinese in 1921. The Mongolian People's Republic was officially proclaimed in Outer, or northern, Mongolia in November 1924, but Inner, or southern, Mongolia remained part of China.

TURKIC ANIMAL STONE CARVING.

Like most Mongolian cities, the hillsides around Uliastay are dotted with *ger* communities. In one *ger* district, north of the centre, was a newly-built Buddhist temple; visual evidence that religion – ruthlessly suppressed during the communist era, when most of Mongolia's monasteries were destroyed – is reviving.

The next leg of our journey took us over the spectacular Zagastain Pass through the Hangai Nuruu, the second largest mountain range in Mongolia. Stopping at its crest our drivers walked three times round a large cairn, adding more stones to the pile, which also included rusting tin cans, animal bones, empty bottles, and had pieces of iron piping with strips of torn cloth tied to them stuck out at crazy angles. This, we were told was an *ovoo* – a kind of shaman shrine, and the ritual meant to ensure us a safe journey.

Shamanism is an ancient religious cult based on the belief that certain people – shamans – can serve as intermediaries between the secular and sacred realms. Shamans once had considerable influence among the nomadic tribes of the steppes, acting as traditional healers, judges and priests, and shamanism remained the main religion of Mongolia until the sixteenth century. In their drive for empire, the Mongols came in contact with other religions – Islam in the West, and Buddhism in the East – which slowly established their ascendancy over the conquerors. The Golden Horde of the Volga and the Il-Khan Mongols in Persia became Muslims, followed somewhat later by the Chagatai Khans of Central Asia. The Mongol Yuan dynasty in China adopted Buddhism, and in Mongolia itself Lamaism – a strain of Buddhism coupled with Shamanism – became the main religion. Today Shamanism is a marginal cult, although some of the superstitions surrounding it are widespread.

Descending Zagastain Pass, we drove along the fertile Ider Gol river valley populated by semi-sedentary nomads, who in addition to *ger* encampments and free-grazing herds had more permanent structures, including animal stockades and log cabins in which they kept animal skins and stores. There were also many signs of past habitation: *kurgans*, earth and stone mounds, some 10 metres (30 feet) high and 30 metres (90 feet) wide, were erected over ancient graves of the nomadic aristocracy.

Excavation of *kurgans* in recent decades has thrown new light on the life of the early nomad. The most remarkable of these finds was discovered in a set of *kurgans* at Pazyryk in the Altai region of Siberia. Although they had been pillaged in ancient times, the permafrost that formed when they were exposed to the air preserved objects that normally would have rotted in the earth, including a large collection of cloth, felt, wood and leather artefacts – among them Persian pile carpets and delicate Chinese silks. These finds are probably a result of 'relay trade' – passed from hand to hand by nomadic tribes – or perhaps of booty taken by nomad raiders.

THE COLLAPSIBLE FELT YURT (ABOVE), ONCE WIDESPREAD ON THE EURASIAN STEPPE, IS STILL USED AS A DWELLING TODAY BY THIS SEMI-NOMADIC KAZAK COMMUNITY NEAR HOVD IN WESTERN MONGOLIA. ALTHOUGH THE EXTERIOR, WITH THE EXCEPTION OF THE DOOR (RIGHT), IS DRAB, THE INSIDE IS COSY AND CHEERFUL (ABOVE RIGHT).

The expansion of the Hsiung-nu empire significantly increased trade and other contacts between East and West. A route became active leading from the west through the oases of Central Asia to the Hsiung-nu's headquarters in Mongolia and then southward to China. Along this road artistic products of the Hellenic Near East were delivered to the Hunnic aristocracy, while wool fabrics, tapestries and embroideries were brought from Sogdiana, Greek Bactria and Syria. Meanwhile from the Han Empire to the south came silk cloth and lacquerware.

Chinese silk was first carried to the Eurasian hinterland by migrating nomadic tribes such as the Yue-chi retreating westward before the pressure of the Hun, and from there spread to Europe via the Sythians. Silk fabrics and silk fringes sewn on to woollen garments have also been found in sixth- and fifth-century B.C. graves in Greece, Germany and Luxembourg.

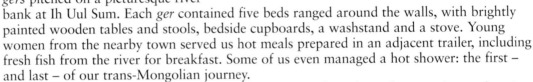

We spent the next two nights in comparative luxury – at a encampment of traditional Mongolian *gers* pitched on a picturesque river bank at Ih Uul Sum. Each *ger* contained five beds ranged around the walls, with brightly painted wooden tables and stools, bedside cupboards, a washstand and a stove. Young women from the nearby town served us hot meals prepared in an adjacent trailer, including fresh fish from the river for breakfast. Some of us even managed a hot shower: the first – and last – of our trans-Mongolian journey.

For entertainment there was a travelling circus: students from the state circus, changing in a battered bus and performing on a large carpet laid out in a nearby forest clearing. Acrobats, jugglers, clowns, a trick cyclist and a magician who produced a contortionist from a mini-*ger* enthralled an audience of wide-eyed children and bemused grown-ups from the nearby town.

Our stay at Ih Uul Sum was all too brief, and soon we were battling sleet and icy winds through the steep Solongat Pass. We spent a cold and hungry night by Terhiin Tsagaan Nuur Lake, when the baggage truck with our extra clothing and our incredible mobile kitchen failed to arrived – they had got stuck in swollen stream – forcing us to light fires to keep warm, and break into our emergency supplies of dried fruit and nuts.

Although our itinerary called for another night under canvas by Terhiin Tsagaan Nuur, we moved next day into the nearby town of Horgo, taking over whatever accommodation

*NEXT SPREAD
THE NOMADIC
TRADITIONS OF STEPPE
PEOPLES GIVES RISE TO
A COLOURFUL EQUINE
CULTURE. HERE
MONGOLIAN BOY
JOCKEYS ARE ESCORTED
ACROSS THE FINISHING
LINE AT THE END OF A
GRUELLING
MARATHON.*

we could find. Our enterprising driver, Monku, found Wheeler and me a room in a primitive hotel. It had outdoor pit toilets and no running water, but it was warm, and at the equivalent of 70 US cents a night – for the both of us – was a bargain.

Emerging next day from the Hangai range, we reached Tsetserleg, one of the few Mongolian cities that can be called picturesque. Situated on a grassy plateau 1,695 metres (5,085 feet) above sea level, it grew up around Zay Monastery. The first temple was built in 1586, and later expanded in 1679 to five. Today most of them serve as a museum complex, which presumably is what saved them from destruction in the Stalinist purges. One temple however is again a place of worship, and prayers were in progress when we arrived.

We strolled through the street market at Tsetserleg but there was precious little to buy. For more than a generation, Moscow

subsidized Mongolia as a military buffer against China, but with the disintegration of the Soviet Union these subsidies ceased, plunging Mongolia into economic chaos.

I did buy a large hand-made metal ladle to make bathing in rivers easier, but it was much too cold that evening to even think about bathing in the river at Undursant beside which we pitched our tents. Instead we watched a dazzling display of equestrianism, as local herders rounded up horses scattered across surrounding grasslands.

Steppe peoples are horse riders par excellence. Their military strategy was based entirely on equestrian manoeuvres. At the same time they perfected the art of archery, and were sometimes referred to as the 'archer tribes'. Their dress was appropriate for riding – jackets, trousers and leather knee boots giving them the freedom of movement to gallop and manoeuvre.

By the fifth century, horse-riding Turkic tribes controlled much of the steppe, carving out a huge nomad empire stretching from their homeland in Mongolia as far west as the Black Sea. The Turks made their headquarters in the Orhon Valley, a traditional seat of steppe power along which we now made our way to the ruins of Karabalgasun. This was Mongolia's first walled city, built by the Uighur Turks as their capital after they emerged victorious from a power struggle among the tribes of the Turkic empire in 745. Karabalgasun was sacked by another Turkic people, the Kyrgyz, in 840, but its ruined fortifications still dwarf the surrounding grasslands. The stone pillars, marble carvings and ceramic tiles found there indicate the Uighurs enjoyed a standard of living unparalleled in medieval Central Asia.

The Mongols too built their capital in the Orhon Valley, about 40 kilometres (25 miles) downriver from Karabalgasun, near the present-day town of Harhorin, and we too made our headquarters there for the next few days. Construction of Karakoram began during the reign of Ogodeï Khan (1229–41), but it was not until the reign of Möngke Khan (1251–9) that the city became the true centre of the Mongol empire. It was a cosmopolitan city, where one could meet Muslims, Christians and Buddhists, Arabs, Chinese and Europeans, for besides being the administrative centre of the Mongolian empire, it was also a commercial crossroads of the Silk Roads.

Contemporary travel accounts give lively descriptions of Karakoram. Friar William of Rubruck, ambassador of the French King Louis IX, who visited Mongolia in the thirteenth century, was greatly impressed by the Khan's palace and a large tree at its entrance made of silver. He writes in his book, *Travel to the East*, that the palace resembled a church, with a middle nave and two sides beyond two rows of pillars. The silver tree, made by William Buchier, a Parisian sculptor living in Karakoram, 'had at its roots four lions of silver, all belching forth white mares' milk ... and gilded serpents, twined round the tree, from which flowed wine, *caracosmos*, or clarified mares' milk, *bal*, a drink made with honey, and rice mead'.

In the treetop, reported Rubruck,

is an angel holding a trumpet, and underneath the tree a vault in which a man hid. Outside the palace is a cellar in which the liquors are stored, and where there are servants all ready to pour them out. When drink is wanted, the head butler cries to the angel to blow his trumpet, and he who is concealed in the vault, hearing this, blows the trumpet right loudly. The servants in the cellar, hearing the trumpet, pour the different liquors into the proper conduits, and the conduits carry them down into bowls at the foot of the tree from where the butlers draw it and carry it to the palace.

THE ENORMOUS WALLED MONASTERY OF ERDENE ZUU AT KARAKORAM, THIRTEENTH-CENTURY CAPITAL OF THE MONGOL EMPIRE AND COMMERCIAL CROSSROADS OF THE STEPPE ROUTE.

The palace of the Khan and his Mongol entourage was surrounded by a high wall and stood apart from the city, which had two quarters: one for Muslims, where there were bazaars and many traders gathered, and the other for the Chinese, who were mostly craftspeople. There were also large palaces belonging to the court secretaries, and twelve Buddhist temples, two mosques and a Christian church. The city was surrounded by a mud wall and had four gates. At the eastern gate, wheat and cereals were sold; at the western gate, sheep and goats; at the southern gate, oxen and wagons were on sale; and at the northern gate, horses.

Nothing now remains of the ancient city of Karakoram, which at its zenith had a population of 10,000, save a few scattered stones and a stele inscribed with Arabic verse from the *Koran*. The stele is believed to be from one of Karakoram's two mosques, which during the thirteenth century served the city's Muslim community. Muslim merchants from Persia and Central Asia were active traders throughout the Mongol Empire. The Mongol and Turkic nomads served mostly as caravan drivers and guides, and supplied the merchants with camels and horses, and food and lodgings all along their route.

The Mongols created a new road across Eurasia – the Mongol Way. A horse relay post road that ran in its Central Asian part parallel to the Silk Road, it linked Mongolia with Europe. The system was based on a series of relay stations, which held stocks of horses and fodder at stages equivalent to a day's journey: about 40 to 50 kilometres (25 to 30 miles). The main West–East route began in Mongol-ruled territories in Russia, and proceeded east across the steppe north of the Aral Sea and south of Lake Balkash. Crossing the Chu and Ili rivers, it then proceeded through the Altai and Hangai Mountains to Karakoram, the capital of the Mongol empire – a distance of some 4,800 kilometres (3,000 miles).

In the thirteenth century, Kublai Khan (1260–94), a grandson of Genghis Khan, conquered China, and moved his capital to Khanbalik, on the site of present-day Beijing. Mongolia itself reverted to a collection of feudal fiefdoms, and it was after this that Karakoram fell into decline. On its ruins, however, arose one of the most spectacular sights of the steppe – the immense walled monastery of Erdene Zuu.

Although most of its temples have been destroyed, the massive wall linking over 100 monumental *stupas* still surrounds the 400 metre (1,200 feet) compound in which they once stood. Established by the Mongolian prince Avtay Khan in 1586, construction continued up to the beginning of the nineteenth century in a mixture of Mongolian, Tibetan and Chinese architectural styles. At its height, the monastery had 100 temples and over 1,000 monks, but during the Stalinist purges of the 1930s all but three of the temples were destroyed and the monks dispersed. The monastery remained closed until 1965, when it was reopened as a museum. It became active as a monastery again in 1990, when religious freedom was restored.

Spaced evenly along each of its four walls are twenty-five *stupas*, plus double *stupas* on each corner, making 108 in all. In the northwest corner of the immense walled compound are the three temples that survived the purge. Each contains large statues of Buddha and his disciples, plus bells, kettledrums, prayer wheels, perfume pans and other Buddhist paraphernalia.

In the centre of the compound a circular stone floor – 20 metres (60 feet) in diameter – is all that is left of a huge *ger* set up in 1658 for a congress of all Mongol khans. In the southwest section of the compound stands the recently restored, and once more active, Lavran Lamasery – the only monument of Tibetan architectural style preserved in Mongolia. In contrast to the sweeping roofs of the monastery's three Chinese-style temples, the Tibetan-style lamasery is flat-roofed and fortress-like. Instead of green tiles and griffins, its exterior is white and adorned with gold plaques and plaster skulls.

It was from here one morning that we watched the start of a colourful,

BUDDHISM BECAME ACTIVE AGAIN IN MONGOLIA IN 1990 WHEN RELIGIOUS FREEDOM WAS RESTORED FOLLOWING THE COLLAPSE OF COMMUNISM IN CENTRAL ASIA.

TRADITIONAL MONGOLIAN HEADDRESS.

carnival-like Buddhist procession dedicated – appropriately for Mongolia's equine culture – to Buddha's horse. It involved hauling a huge replica of a horse around the perimeter of the monastery, preceded by animal-like figures and accompanied by much clashing of cymbals, banging of drums and blowing of trumpets by lamas in yellow caps and red robes. It was, we were told, only the fourth time in fifty-three years this ceremony had been performed, and it attracted several hundred people from the nearby Harhorin.

We eventually caught up with Genghis Khan – or at least a lookalike – in Ulan Bator, the coldest capital on earth. It was at the Nadaam Festival, marking the end of the harsh winter when temperatures plunge to -25 °C, and the onset of spring. During communist rule all discussion of Genghis Khan was outlawed, but with the switch to democracy the ban was lifted, and that day his lookalike was leading the Nadaam parade.

In legend the offspring of a deer and a wolf, but in reality the orphaned son of a Mongol chieftain, Genghis Khan began his career as a conqueror by subduing the tribes he blamed for his father's murder. By 1206 he had welded all the tribes of Mongolia into a single confederacy and forged their cavalry into a formidable war machine.

MONGOL WARRIORS WORE MAIL ARMOUR AND HELMETS. A COMPOUND BOW WAS THEIR PRIMARY WEAPON, AND ARCHERY AS WELL AS OTHER MARTIAL ARTS SUCH AS WRESTLING REMAIN IMPORTANT AS SPORTS IN MONGOLIA TODAY.

In 1218 Genghis Khan unleashed 200,000 men against the Mongols' western neighbours, the Khorezmshahs, in retaliation for the murder of 450 merchants en route from Mongolia and the theft of their goods by the Khorezmian governor of Otrar. Soon all of Central Asia and Persia had felt the wrath of the Mongols as they pursued the fleeing shah of Khorezm, Muhammad, as far as the Caspian Sea.

Before he died, Genghis Khan divided his dominions between his four sons, with overall leadership going to Ogodeï, who inherited the Mongol heartland of western Mongolia. Tolui was awarded eastern Mongolia, Jochi received the Western Steppe, and Chaghataï obtained what is now Uzbekistan and northern Iran. Genghis Khan's sons conquered China, Eastern Europe and the Middle East. At its zenith their empire was one of the largest the world has ever known – stretching from the Pacific in the east to the Danube in the west, and from Siberia in the north to Burma in the south.

The Mongols' conquests were of a scope and range never equalled, and had a tremendous impact on world history. The political organization of Asia and a large part of Europe was altered; whole peoples were uprooted and dispersed, permanently changing the ethnic character of many regions, and the strength and distribution of the principal religions of the world were decisively altered.

The Mongols ruled their massive empire by force, imposing within its borders a respect for law that was absolute, so that, the saying goes, 'a girl could walk across it from one end to the other bearing a golden dish on her head without being molested'. Although history remembers them as marauders, it was during this so-called 'Mongol Peace' and under Mongol protection that European merchants – among them Marco Polo – were safely able to traverse the normally unruly steppes; establishing direct contact between China and the West for the very first time.

THE IMPERIAL HIGHWAY

Carrying silk and jade, we set off like the traders of old along the southern rim of the Heavenly Mountains, on the last leg of our journey along the Silk Roads. But we were carrying souvenirs, not merchandise, and we were travelling not by camel but by jet.

Xinjiang's forbidding no man's land between west and east might almost have been designed expressly as a barrier by nature; except by air, it is almost as difficult to cross today as it was in ancient times. To the east are the Lop and Gobi Deserts, to the north, south and west the Tian Shan, Kunlun, Pamir and Karakoram ranges, while the central Tarim Basin is for the most part covered by the shifting sands of the Taklamakan Desert.

Nearly 1,000 kilometres (620 miles) across, east to west, and 400 kilometres (250 miles) from north to south, the Taklamakan's red-gold dunes tower as high as 100 metres (325 feet). Driven by relentless winds, they are said to have buried without trace caravans, armies and towns. Although some of these terrible tales were undoubtedly spread by merchants seeking to deter competition, few travellers have ever had a good word to say about the Taklamakan.

The ancient Chinese believed the desert was inhabited by demons and evil spirits which lured travellers to a thirsty grave; the modern Chinese use it for testing nuclear weapons. Marco Polo wrote of terrifying mirages – 'hosts of men coming toward them' – which caused merchants, 'suspecting they were robbers', to take flight and lose their way; modern Swedish explorer Sven Hedin called it 'the most dangerous desert in the world'.

Because there was no safe way across this deadly dustbowl, the Silk Road skirted it warily. After descending the precipitous defiles of the 'Roof of the World' to Kashgar, it divided around the fringes of the Taklamakan, where the occasional glacier-fed river made human habitation possible.

The route south of the Taklamakan followed the foothills of the Karakoram range to the oasis of Yarkand, and continued east along the fringe of the Kunlun Mountains to the ancient jade market of Khotan. The northern route followed the foothills of the Tian Shan to Kucha before descending into one of the deepest – and hottest – depressions on earth, to the surprisingly bountiful oasis of Turpan. Here, 154 metres (500 feet) below sea level, in ovenlike temperatures of 40 °C (104 °F) and watered by a mere 16 millimetres (five-eighths of an inch) of rain a year, a bastion of civilization thrived in which religions and cultures coexisted, and literature and art flourished.

Turpan's secret was a network of hand-dug gravity tunnels that carried melted snow from the nearby Tian Shan range. Even today this centuries-old system supports a sizeable city surrounded by fertile farmland that produces grapes prized throughout China, and irrigates verdant stands of elm, poplar and palm that keep the desert at bay.

Turpan oasis has been famous for its grapes for more than 2,000 years. They were part of its tribute to the Chinese emperor during the Tang dynasty – sent east along the Silk

A CHINESE-STYLE PAGODA (LEFT) AND PAVILION (ABOVE) ATOP RED HILL AT URUMCHI, LEAVE NO DOUBT THAT THE CHINESE ARE NOW IN CHARGE OF THIS TRADITIONALLY UIGHUR CITY.

Road, packed in lead-lined boxes between layers of snow from the Tian Shan, to the court of Xian. Today, Turpan still lives in the dappled shade of its vines. Trellises span everything: streets, courtyards and even roofless rooms where families sleep outdoors on balmy summer nights.

Turpan has always been an important centre of administration and trade. Here, Han emperors established the military base of Jiaohe to defend China's borderlands and protect its trade with the West. Jiaohe was a natural fortress, a citadel built on a small island left between two rivers when melting snows from Tian Shan glaciers gouged out deep ravines. With cliffs 20 to 30 metres high (65 to 100 feet) on either side, Jiaohe did not even need a city wall. During the Han dynasty 1,000 troops were stationed here, and by the eighth century Jiaohe supported a population of 7,000. But then, as the climate became drier and the river's flow more scant, the citadel was gradually abandoned.

Today Jiaohe still stands, a silent, ghostly warren of adobe walls, preserved by the very dryness that brought its demise. Close inspection of these seemingly random shapes reveals clearly defined streets and houses laid out in grid fashion: a lifesize model of a city constructed 2,000 years ago.

Turpan oasis is also the site of the ruins of Gaochang, capital of the Uighur kingdom of Khocho, which flourished in Xinjiang from the ninth to the thirteenth century. This city, which was an important staging post on the Silk Roads, supported a multiracial, multilingual population of 30,000 and was ringed by an imposing wall 12 metres (39 feet) thick and 6 kilometres (3.7 miles) long, much of which is still standing.

The Uighurs once ruled Mongolia, built its first walled cities and created its first literate civilization. But in 840 another Turkic people, the Kirgiz, drove them southwest to Xinjiang, where they established the kingdom of Khocho and inhabited the oasis towns through which passed the ancient Silk Roads. Today, the Uighurs are still the predominant people of Xinjiang, where they maintain their own language, an ancient form of modern Turkish, and their own religion, Islam. Uighur men still proudly wear traditional skullcaps and Uighur women can still be distinguished from the Han Chinese who have moved into the area, not only by their features, but by their brightly coloured chiffon headscarves.

Having crossed the Taklamakan by air, we rejoined the Silk Road at Urumqi, the world's most landlocked city. Farther than any other from the open sea, it is today the capital of the Xinjiang Uighur autonomous region. China's government has done much to modernize Urumqi in recent years, building factories, hospitals and hotels. A raw colonial outpost when I first visited it in 1984, it is now a modern metropolis with high-rise apartment buildings, factories, and even a five-star hotel. Skyscrapers have sprouted in the centre, and the streets are choked with traffic.

The majority of people living in Urumqi are now Han Chinese, but outside the capital Uighurs are still predominant. And although Urumqi has changed beyond recognition, the oases of the Tarim Basin still have a distinctive Central Asian flavour. Here donkey carts are still the main form of transportation, women cook on open fires in

FARMERS WINNOWING WHEAT WITHIN THE RUINS OF GAOCHANG, CAPITAL OF THE ANCIENT UIGHUR KINGDOM OF KHOCHO, IN WESTERN CHINA.

A GIRL EMBROIDERS A TRADITIONAL UYGUR SKULLCAP.

walled courtyards of mudbrick homes, and boys and girls in baggy pants dance to the wailing clarinet and heavy beat of drums.

Although relatively small in number compared with the Han Chinese, who make up 93 per cent of China's 1.2 billion population, Xinjiang's Muslims are politically significant because they occupy vast, strategically important borderlands that are rich in natural resources vital to the development of modern China. Predominantly Muslim Xinjiang, for example, which, with an area of 1,646,700 square kilometres (635,800 square miles) covers one-sixth of China's land area, borders Afghanistan, India, Mongolia and Pakistan, plus the former Soviet republics of Kazakstan, Kirgizia and Tajikstan, and is believed to have one of the world's largest unexploited deposits of oil and gas.

The open-door polices that are spectacularly transforming China's coastal regions are bringing change to the country's vast landlocked northwest, too. But here, far from the economic boom along the coast, the changes are coming only gradually – and with complications, for compounding the problem of economic unevenness is simmering ethnic strife. Of Xinjiang's 15 million people, over 8 million are Muslims related to the Turkic peoples of Central Asia.

Ethnic tensions have simmered for decades in northwest China, many of whose people share a culture, language and blood ties with the peoples across its borders. These borders are porous both for goods that are found in local bazaars and for ideas.

THE ABANDONED SILK ROAD GARRISON OF JIAOHE, BUILT BY THE CHINESE TO PROTECT THEIR WESTERN BORDERLANDS AND SAFEGUARD TRADE WITH THE WEST.

Along the Silk Road, the nearness of the mountains with their gorges caused local Buddhists and their patrons to carve community buildings and halls of worship out of the cliff walls. In other words they built and decorated cave temples, accessible by artificially built steps. Thriving schools of Buddhist learning sprang up in the oasis cities and garrison towns along the Silk Road. Under the patronage of local rulers and the religious community, great programmes of Buddhist subject matter were painted in glorious colours on the walls of cave temples and monasteries.

The vitality of religious centres, like that of Silk Road cities and oases themselves, depended on commerce. With the collapse of East–West overland trade, monasteries, temples, mosques and madrasa were abandoned and fell into ruin. Many religious sites in Eastern Turkestan were covered by desert sands and remained hidden until their rediscovery at the beginning of this century.

Preserved from destruction by the dry climate, and immured in hiding places where they were concealed at the approach of invaders, thousands of manuscripts found in these centres bear witness to the power of the religious currents that passed along the Silk Road; recapturing the faith of disciples of a triumphant religion or of a religion seeking refuge from persecution elsewhere, of a religion still dominant today or one now almost extinct.

The Manichaean faith was founded in the third century in Mesopotamia by Mani (216–76), who threaded together elements of Christianity, Judaism and Zoroastrianism into a new religion. It was spread by Manichaean missionaries to North Africa in the west and China in the east. In 762 the khan of the Uighurs, a Turkic people living on the Mongolian steppe, converted to this religion and made Manichaeism the state religion of his steppe kingdom.

The Manichaean Uighur state was shattered in 840 when another Turkic people, the Kyrgyz, invaded Uighur lands. Many Uighurs fled south, seeking refuge in the oasis towns of the Silk Road in present-day Xinjiang and along the Gansu Corridor in China. It was in the oasis of Turfan that Uighur princes established a kingdom called Khocho (850–1250). Up to the beginning of the eleventh century, many rulers of that kingdom were Manichaeans. Manichaean learning and art flourished, with many wealthy donors giving the means to copy documents and create new works of art.

Although Uighur rulers adopted the Manichaean religion, and Nestorian Christianity gained a foothold in Turpan, Xinjiang's masses were Buddhist until, beginning in the tenth century, the entire population converted to Islam. So complete, in fact, was the eclipse of these pre-Islamic cultures that it was not until the start of the twentieth century that their past existence in this remote part of the world was rediscovered. In mountain gorges along the Silk Roads where local Buddhists carved out and decorated cave temples in cliff walls, archaeologists discovered magnificent frescoes and libraries. They also found priceless relics of Manichaean and Nestorian literature.

These finds spurred a great rush of treasure hunters, who cut from cave walls frescoes that had survived 1,000 years and sent them to 'safety' in western Europe and Japan. Many of them perished when the Berlin Ethnological Museum was destroyed by Allied bombing in the Second World War. Some of those responsible for these archaeological thefts were, like me, British – and the only time I felt myself the object of any animosity during my many visits to China was when the guardian of the looted cave monastery of Bezeklik, near Turpan, pointed accusingly at the sites of missing frescoes and, scowling, said, 'Stolen!'

It took two nights and a day to cross the bleak wilderness where the two great deserts of Asia – the Taklamakan and the Gobi – meet; travelling in a scheduled Chinese passenger train pulled by a shiny black 133-ton, 2,500-horsepower steam locomotive, its six driving wheels painted bright red and edged with white. About 7,000 steam locomotives still ply the rails in China, pulling 70 per cent of the country's freight and 60 per cent of its passengers – and that means three million people a day.

Soft class – a carpeted corridor car with private sleeping compartments done in white

THE GREAT WALL, WHICH SNAKES 2,400 KILOMETRES (1,500 MILES) ACROSS NORTHWEST CHINA, IS THE ONLY MAN-MADE STRUCTURE VISIBLE FROM OUTER SPACE.

© UNESCO

linen – was almost empty. Hard class – bare dormitory carriages – was packed to overflowing. But the Chinese, untroubled by the lack of privacy, were making a party of it, playing cards, sharing food and swapping stories. I swapped a copy of an American magazine for a battered edition of the comic-strip adventures of the Belgian boy reporter Tintin – in Chinese.

Sometime during the second night we slipped past Anxi, where the Silk Roads north and south of the Taklamakan rejoin to course eastward through the Yumen Pass, and past the impressive Oriental ramparts of the western end of the Great Wall into China proper. The great Ming fortress of Jiayuguan was the last bastion of the Great Wall, which curves across the width of the Gobi. Three elaborately decorated pavilions perch improbably above the battlements which marked what was once the end of China. It was from here that caravans once struck out for Central Asia.

Significantly, our word 'China' comes from Qin (pronounced 'chin'), the name of the dynasty that first united China and linked up a series of earlier bulwarks to form the Great Wall. Generally acknowledged as one of the wonders of the world, the Great Wall snakes back and forth for 2,400 kilometres (1,500 miles) across northwestern China, effectively separating the settled and cultivated lands of China from the nomadic herdspeople without. It was not, however, impermeable. In a major offensive around 200 B.C. the Hsiung-nu, or Huns, broke through the wall, and it was not until the middle of the first century A.D. that the Chinese succeeded in driving them back. But it was not the last the world had heard of the Hsiung-nu: remnants of these fierce archer tribes moved west, and their descendants, the Huns, united under Attila to terrorize central Europe from A.D. 434 to 453.

Once we were inside the protection of the Great Wall, the going was fairly easy: a paved road, the Imperial Highway, follows the 1,200 kilometre (740 mile) Gansu Corridor, caught between the Gobi Desert and the Qilian Mountains. Then and now there was a natural link between China's western borderlands and the Yellow River (Huang Ho) valley, birthplace of Chinese civilization.

It was along the Yellow River in north-central China that, according to historians, Neolithic farmers first discovered sericulture – the art of rearing silkworms for thread – about 4,000 years ago. Legend, however, places the event even earlier and credits Xiling Shi, wife of Huangdi, the semi-mythical emperor who ruled China in the middle of the third millennium B.C., with the discovery of silk thread. According to the legend, Xiling Shi was strolling in the palace garden one day and passed under a mulberry tree, from one of whose leaves she idly plucked a white cocoon. Later, as she took tea, she accidentally dropped the cocoon into her steaming cup, and reaching in to fish it out, unravelled a long white thread.

Whatever the case, silk has been an important part of China's economy and culture for as long as anyone can remember – and remains so still. Silk to begin with was reserved exclusively for the use of the ruler, his close relations and the very highest of his officials. Under the Han dynasty silk began to be used for paying civil servants and rewarding subjects for outstanding services to the state.

CHINA'S YELLOW RIVER VALLEY, WHERE SERICULTURE – THE ART OF RAISING SILK WORMS FOR THREAD – WAS FIRST DEVELOPED ABOUT 4,000 YEARS AGO.

SILKWORMS FEEDING ON MULBERRY LEAVES WHILE SPINNING A COCOON.

© UNESCO/X.KAIXUAN

Taxes were paid in lengths of silk, and before long it was to become a currency used in trade with foreign countries. Silk was also used by Han rulers as diplomatic gifts and to buy off the troublesome nomads of the north. By the time of the Han dynasty, the place of silk in China's economy and culture was securely established, as were the complex methods of its cultivation and manufacture. They have changed little since.

The silkworm caterpillar is the larva of *Bombyx mori*, a heavy flightless moth. Glands in the caterpillar's head secrete silk thread, and moving in a figure of eight pattern, the larva lays thread upon thread to build an oval cocoon. Only enough moths are allowed to hatch to lay the next generation of eggs. The rest of the cocoons are steamed to kill the pupa and then sorted, with only the whitest and most perfect being set aside for silk.

Some 1.5 kilometres (0.94 miles) of silk filament can be unwound from a single cocoon, but the material is so fine that as many as nine cocoon filaments are needed to produce a single silk thread. For the peoples of Central Asia and farther west, silk was a miraculous fabric: light and strong, glossy and dirt-resistant, susceptible to subtle dyeing and extremely long-lasting. How it was made and what it was made of were mysteries, adding to its allure.

Silk was a symbol of royalty, wealth and power, and of all the goods produced in China it was the one that Western merchants sought before all others. So important was silk to the economy that the process of making it was guarded in ancient China as carefully as nations today guard their atomic secrets. Exporting the eggs of the silkworm or the seeds of the mulberry tree was punishable by death, and visiting foreigners were kept away from silkworm nurseries and mulberry tree plantations. Because of this, sericulture remained a mystery to the West for centuries.

Eventually, however, the secret leaked out. One famous fable recounts that a Chinese princess, married off to the King of Khotan, smuggled silkworms hidden in her hair past Chinese frontier guards. British archaeologist Sir Aurel Stein found a fresco depicting this princess near Khotan – implying that the woman who betrayed China's best-kept secret was a heroine to the Khotanese – and documents unearthed at Turpan confirm that sericulture existed there in the fifth century.

The technique of silk weaving quickly spread throughout Central Asia, and by the sixth century had reached Persia. In the seventh and eighth centuries Central Asia developed its own silk industry, incorporating elements of local, Iranian and Chinese design in patterned fabrics. By the time of Emperor Justinian the Byzantine world was able not only to cultivate silkworms but also to produce silk fabrics and export them. Over the following centuries, the secrets of silk production spread rapidly to a number of European countries.

Despite its production in numerous countries today, and despite competition from artificial fibres, Chinese silk is still prized throughout the world, and remains one of China's most prestigious exports: 9,300 tons of natural silk, 70,000,000 metres (75,000,000 yards) of silk garments and 150,000,000 metres (162,500,000 yards) of unsown silk cloth are sold abroad each year. The cloth alone would reach four times around the Earth, or more than fifteen times the entire length of our journey along the Silk Roads.

China itself is not immune to the mystique of the Silk Roads. At Lanzhou, a former staging post on the Yellow River, we watched the Song and Dance Ensemble of Gansu Province rehearsing a popular ballet entitled *Tales of the Silk Road*. It is based on stories told in 45,000 square metres (11 acres) of paintings on the walls of 492 caves carved out

MEMBERS OF THE SONG AND DANCE ENSEMBLE OF GANSU REHEARSING THE BALLET TALES OF THE SILK ROAD.

*Big Wild Goose
Pagoda, built in
Xian to house
rare Buddhist
scripts brought
from China
along the
Silk Road.*

of a cliff face at Dunhuang, undoubtedly the most important Silk Road Buddhist centre. The caves were decorated by monks between the fourth and fourteenth centuries. Here too, a walled-up library was discovered at the beginning of the twentieth century, where manuscripts were stored that together weighed a ton.

Whole monasteries were carved out of the soft cliffs, and on their walls is the greatest collection of Buddhist painting in the world. Spanning 1,000 years, the rock temples are crowded with musicians, flying angels, noblemen in gaudy robes and sexual acrobats, beneath the complacent gaze of smiling Buddhas. These works are the product of a remarkable Silk Road civilization which, until its rediscovery at the end of the nineteenth century, had dropped from historical sight.

In Lanzhou we slept in the Communist Party guesthouse – more comfortable than most hotels in China. After centuries of stagnation, Lanzhou is experiencing an economic revival as both an industrial and – once more – a communication centre. The extension of the railroad to Urumqi and beyond has again made Lanzhou an important staging post for the northwest.

Back on the train, we made the final run to Xian across the fertile Shaanxi plain, its luxuriant patchwork of green and yellow fields a stark contrast to the harsh landscapes of Xinjiang and Gansu. Every now and then we passed farmers in lampshade hats stacking grain. in sheaves covered with straw 'hats' of the same shape to protect them from the rain.

Our train skirted the rectangular city wall of Xian – 14 kilometres (9 miles) long, and in the city's great days, wide enough to allow two-way chariot traffic along its top – then cut through a breach to the central station. Once China's entry point for new ideas and new technology, Xian too is experiencing a revival as thousands of foreigners once more beat a track through its imposing city gates, following the discovery nearby of the life-size, 6,000 man terracotta army buried 2,200 years ago to guard the tomb of Emperor Qin Shi Huangdi, first unifier of China.

Formerly Ch'ang-an, 'City of Eternal Peace' and capital of eleven dynasties, Xian was the eastern terminus of the Silk Roads for 1,100 years – a great cosmopolitan city where merchants from every land rubbed shoulders and struck deals. Once one of the most important cities in the world, Xian's population in the seventh century topped 2 million, including large communities of foreign traders – among them Muslims who built China's biggest mosque.

Laid out Chinese style among gracious gardens and elegantly eaved pavilions, Xian's Great Mosque stands amid the neat white houses and narrow lanes of the Muslim quarter. The prayer hall resembles a Ming temple from outside, but retains the indispensable aspects of a mosque within. A mosque serving Muslim merchants has stood on this site since the eighth century. Muslims have always found ways to worship in China, building their mosques to blend with the predominant Buddhist and Taoist sanctuaries, demonstrating the historical ability of Islam to adapt – and survive – in varied religious and political climates.

Today Xian's Muslim citizens, some of them descendants of traders on the Silk Roads, still pray in that mosque, and their restaurants and shops add flavour to the city. In the streets there are still tantalising echoes of the Silk Road, and the call of the muezzin coming from above the narrow lanes of the Muslim quarter evokes the places at the other end of the Silk Road.

Suddenly our travels were over, and everything I had been fighting off for the past few weeks – cold, damp and germs – caught up with me. As I lay recuperating in a darkened hotel room in Hong Kong, I recalled Marco Polo's deathbed assertion to those who insisted he retract his unbelievable and apparently fantastic stories of far-off lands.

He replied, 'I have not told half of what I saw.'

And neither have I.

THE GRAND MOSQUE IN XIAN, BUILT TWELVE CENTURIES AGO TO SERVE MUSLIM MERCHANTS, HAS ELABORATELY FLARED EAVES TYPICAL OF A CHINESE PAGODA.

THE SPICE ROUTE

*STRUNG OUT ALONG
THE MALABAR COAST,
CANTILEVERED FISHING NETS
INTRODUCED BY TRADERS
FROM THE COURT OF KUBLAI
KHAN STAND TESTIMONY TO
INDIA'S ANCIENT TRADING
LINKS WITH CHINA.*

Curiosity, commerce, conversion and conquest were the key factors in the movement of people along the world's great sea routes. The most colourful and contentious of all these seaways was the Spice Route, which for over 2,000 years linked East and West across the Indian Ocean.

Ships from many lands sailed the Spice Route, laden with all the exotica of the Orient, but it was the precious spices of South-East Asia that gave the route its name. Although now commonplace, cloves, pepper and nutmeg were once rarities worth their weight in gold. Their lucrative trade bred international rivalries, quarrels and conquests, while the search for their source impelled Columbus to cross the Atlantic and Magellan to circumnavigate the globe.

The Spice Route was not a single route, but a network of sea lanes that joined the Mediterranean with the Far East. It stretched 12,000 kilometres (7,500 miles) across the Near East, and around India to China and the Spice Islands of Indonesia. En route it linked some of the world's most exciting sea ports along its most exotic shores.

Mariners from many nations sailed the Spice Route, and its ports served as melting pots for ideas and information. Three of the world's major religions, Christianity, Buddhism and Islam, spread via the Spice Route, while the commercial enterprises of its European traders eventually emerged as colonial empires. Its name became a sort of shorthand, referring not only to the physical route of the ships, but also to the trade with Asia in general. It was also known as the Maritime Silk Route, for as the overland Silk Route declined, the ships that sailed it increasingly carried as cargo the silk and porcelain of China.

Imported trade goods, such as Chinese porcelain, introduced Western craftspeople to not only new art styles, but also new technologies. Chinese potters developed the process of making porcelain – using kaolin – in the ninth century. Its translucency and thinness gave it great appeal, and potters outside China – unaware of kaolin – went to great lengths to duplicate it. Experiments by European potters eventually led to the unlocking of the secret of kaolin in the late seventeenth century. Once it was known, many ceramic factories produced copies of Chinese ware.

The history of spices can be traced almost to the birth of civilization itself. The world's oldest known recipes, recorded in cuneiform on Akkadian clay tablets about 1700 B.C., show the ancient peoples of Mesopotamia used

a wide range of spices in their cooking: no recipe contains fewer than three condiments, and some contain as many as ten. In earliest times, however, spices were used not so much for seasoning food as for religious purposes, for embalming the dead and for sacrificial and funeral rites. The ancients also used spices in producing medicines, cosmetics and perfumes.

The most prized spice in antiquity was cinnamon. Heavily used by the ancient Egyptians in embalming, it is also mentioned as one of the ingredients of the sacred anointing oil of Hebrew priests (Exodus 30:23), was used by ancient Greeks as a flavour in oils, and sold for the equivalent of US$325 a pound in imperial Rome.

Most spices were indigenous only to certain tropical regions of the Orient. Because they were as high in value as they were low in weight, spices were transported and sold at great profit. All along the route taxes, duties and tolls were levied, so that by the time they reached the West their prices were exorbitant. In the case of some spices, according to the Roman scholar Pliny, their original prices increased a hundredfold.

Two peoples – the Arabs and Indians – stand out as probable founders of the spice trade. Indian sailors shipped Eastern spices west to Arabia, from where the Arabs caravanned them north to Mesopotamia and the Mediterranean. Early trade was essentially a luxury exchange in easily transportable items, and often took the form of gifts or tributes. 'Spices of very great store', for example, were among gifts given to the Hebrew King Solomon by the fabled southwest Arabian Queen of Sheba (1 Kings 10:10) in the ninth century B.C. A century later, according to inscriptions at Nimrud in northern Mesopotamia, 'Mero-dach-baladan of Yakin, king of the Sea Country' – located with near certainty in northeastern Arabia – sent 'spices of all kinds' to the Assyrian monarch Tiglath-Pileser III.

Inevitably these exotic substances found their way to the West, where Greeks and Romans became avid consumers; black pepper from India, for example, was one of the favorite ingredients of Rome's renowned gourmand Apicius, who used it in his celebrated recipe for *locustum elixam cum cuminate* – broiled lobster in cumin sauce. Spices were also in great demand in Rome as salves and charms, as well as for religious and burial rituals.

It was this western craving for spices, and the huge profits to be made from their trade, that laid the basis for the Spice Route, which linked the great civilizations of Europe, India and the Orient for over two millennia. When Near East transit tolls and intermediaries' mark-ups on these goods became prohibitive, they forced the Europeans to look for other routes east – unlocking, in the process, the secret of the Monsoon trade winds, finding a sea route around Africa, and accidentally discovering America.

A STONE CARVING AT BOROBUDUR, INDONESIA, DEPICTING EARLY SOUTHEAST ASIAN MARITIME TRADE.

SPICES ON SALE AT PESHAWAR BAZAAR IN PAKISTAN.

THE RED SEA

It was an ominous start to an eventful journey seasoned with thrills, spills and spice. We were setting out to retrace the Spice Route, which linked the Mediterranean basin and South-East Asia by sea for two millennia, and to visit the remote Spice Islands, Europe's search for which led to discovery of the New World. But driving rain flayed Alexandria's dilapidated docks, where anonymous container cargos have replaced exotic cinnamon and cloves. In the Street of the Mosque of the Spice Traders not a single spice shop still traded.

THE ANCIENT EGYPTIANS WERE AMONG THE FIRST PEOPLES TO USE THE SAIL, AND EVEN TODAY, SAILBOATS PLY THE NILE.

It is difficult today to visualize Alexandria as the glittering western terminal of the fabled Spice Route, or to grasp the importance of spices to the civilizations it served. Although the Spice Islands were once magnets for merchants from all over the world, few people today could distinguish them from Indonesia's 13,000 other tropical isles.

Even the ancient Greeks, who were lavish users of spices, were ignorant of their origin, the historian Herodotus recording in the fifth century B.C. that cinnamon came from remote swamps guarded by monstrous bat-like creatures. This tale, probably spread by intermediaries to protect their earnings from the East–West trade, did not, however, deter ancient mariners from setting out from Egypt to obtain spices direct. So ignoring inauspicious circumstances we too set off by Land Rover along Alexandria's storm-swept corniche road on the first stage of our 12,000 kilometre (7,500 mile) journey which, in three months, would take us up the Nile Valley and across the Arabian Sea, along the coasts of Pakistan and India, down the Malay Peninsula and the length of the Indonesian archipelago to the Spice Islands of Ternate, Tidore, Banda and Ambon.

Our travels, by sea, air, river, road and rail, were the stuff that dreams are made of: ancient wonders of Egypt and the Indian Ocean's exotic shores, idyllic Bali island and South-East Asia's seething cities, plus cultural and culinary delights galore. But they almost ended in disaster when photographer Nik Wheeler plunged headlong down a ravine in Ternate, then fell victim to tropical fever – like many a spice trader of old.

Like the old spice traders too, we put in en route at ports such as Muscat and Malacca, Goa and Galle, over which nations once fought in their fierce struggle for control over the lucrative spice trade. We sneezed our way through ginger and pepper warehouses in Cochin, climbed a nutmeg tree-covered volcano in Banda, and toured a unique clove cigarette factory in Kudus – a town in Indonesia named after Arab Jerusalem and underscoring the long-time Muslim domination of the world's spice trade.

Fascinating though they were, many of the places we visited were but faded reflections of their prosperous past, and none more so than Alexandria. Founded by Alexander the Great in 332 B.C., and capital of Egypt's Greek and Roman overlords for over 1,000 years, virtually nothing remains of the gleaming white marble temples and palaces where Alexander's successors – including Cleopatra – ruled, or of the 120 metre (400 feet) high

Pharos Lighthouse, which was one of the seven wonders of the ancient world. Although Alexandria remains Egypt's largest port and retains some of its Levantine charm – including horse-drawn carriages and elegant cafes – it no longer serves as the centre of commerce from Asia, Africa and Mediterranean Europe, at the crossroads of which it stands.

It was this superb position that made Alexandria the most important entrepôt of the classical world – the western terminus of eastern trade, receiving goods via Red Sea ports from Arabia, India, Africa and South-East Asia for shipment to all parts of the Greek and Roman Empires. But Alexandria was ruined when the bulk of East–West trade shifted from the Red Sea to the Arabian Gulf after the Islamic conquests of the seventh century. It revived in the tenth century when, with the decline of the Abbasid caliphate in Iraq and the rise of the Fatimid dynasty in Egypt, international commerce reverted to the Red Sea. It prospered anew as an entrepôt for the Mediterranean under the Ottoman Turks, who built the medieval fortress that still dominates its harbour, but again lost its place in East–West trade following the discovery of the sea route around Africa to India in 1498.

Despite changing trade patterns, few ports played as important a part in the history of the Spice Route as Alexandria. And so it was from here that we now began our journey.

We drove first across the verdant Nile Delta to the Suez Canal, which today makes it possible for great ships to sail between the Mediterranean and the Red Sea – seemingly, as the level of the water is invisible below the desert, in the sand. Early Spice Route traders, however, had to haul their goods overland from Red Sea ports across the desert by camel caravan to the Nile, then sail them down river to Alexandria. The main Nile terminal for goods coming and going from the Red Sea was Coptus – modern Qift – located where the great eastward curve of the Nile brings it closest to the Red Sea just north of Luxor – the ancient Egyptian capital of Thebes.

As the lower Nile is now no longer navigable, we travelled between Cairo and Luxor by train – a ten-hour journey back 3,500 years in time to the very beginnings of the Spice Route. On the walls of the Pharaonic cemeteries of Thebes is recorded in pictorial relief the story of one of the first expeditions to trade for spice – that of the beautiful young Queen Hatshepsut to the legendary Land of Punt, believed to be either East Africa or Southwest Arabia.

Cinnamon, according to inscriptions on her funerary temple, was one of the 'marvels' brought back to Egypt in 1500 B.C. by galleys despatched by Queen Hatshepsut down the Red Sea to Punt. So we lingered in Luxor to study the story of their voyage, depicted in a series of graphic reliefs decorating the queen's massive three-story mortuary temple, built against a dramatic backdrop of cliffs in the Theban hills.

The Punt reliefs cover the entire wall of the south colonnade of the temple's second terrace, and picture in detail the build and rig of five large Egyptian ships, their arrival in Punt and the loading of their cargos. Further scenes show Queen Hatshepsut announcing the success of the expedition to her officials, and offering the products brought back from Punt to the god Amun.

Queen Hatshepsut's fleet is said to have sailed from Thebes first north down the Nile, then east through an ancient Nile–Suez Canal and finally south down the Red Sea – a detour of some 1,280 kilometres (800 miles). We, however, took the more direct route established by Rameses III about 1175 B.C., and used by Greek, Roman and Arab merchants for over 2,000 years: east overland from Coptus to a port in the region of present-day al-Qusayr, and thence down the Red Sea.

Coptus first developed because of its proximity to the quarries and gold mines of Wadi

ALTHOUGH ONCE THE WESTERN TERMINUS OF THE SPICE ROUTE, NOT A SINGLE SPICE MERCHANT STILL TRADES IN ALEXANDRIA'S STREET OF THE MOSQUE OF THE SPICE TRADERS.

Hammamat, 75 kilometres (47 miles) to its east. The extension of this route to the Red Sea further increased the importance of the town, which flourished until medieval Islamic times, when it was superseded as the Nile terminal for goods and Muslim pilgrims coming and going from the Red Sea by Qus, 10 kilometres (6 miles) upstream.

Today Qift exhibits little evidence of the town's former importance as a river staging post for East–West trade. In fact, the only vessel visible on our visit was a small sail boat waiting to ferry passengers no farther than the opposite bank of the Nile. It is from Qus, still an important Islamic centre, rather than Qift, that the road today strikes out east across the desert and along the Wadi Hammamat to the Red Sea.

THE CAVERNOUS ROMAN WELL AT BIR FAWAKHIR, A MAJOR WATERING STATION FOR CARAVANS PLYING BETWEEN THE NILE RIVER VALLEY AND RED SEA PORTS.

Along this route at last was ample evidence we were travelling an ancient thoroughfare. Ruined Arab watch towers guard its flanks, and at Bir Fawakhir a cavernous Roman well, 6 metres (20 feet) wide and some 80 metres (262 feet) deep – which we descended by a dizzying, 134-step spiral stone staircase – stands testimony to its importance as an age-old watering station. Ancient Egyptian graffiti covering the cliffs where Wadi Hammamat reaches its narrowest point is evidence of caravans resting here as they toiled back to Thebes with the 'marvels' of Punt – among them cinnamon with which to mummify their dead.

But as neither cinnamon trees nor their requisite conditions of soil and climate exist in either East Africa or southwest Arabia, historians have concluded that the spice did not – as the Egyptians believed – originate in Punt, but was brought there from its native Sri Lanka and then transhipped to Egypt. As the Egyptian name for cinnamon, and the names for other items such as peacocks and sandalwood native only to India or places farther east, resemble Tamil words of southern India, it is further assumed they were probably brought to Punt by Indian sailors.

Archaeological evidence indicates that already by 500 B.C. the Near East had become the heart of an extensive trading network, which linked all the major civilizations of antiquity. Located at the heart of this network, the peoples of Arabia – the Gerrhaeans of the northeast, the Sabaeans of the southwest and the Nabateans of the northwest – prospered: buying up cargoes landed on their shores and transhipping them, together with their own products, across the Arabian Peninsula by camel caravan to Mesopotamia and the Mediterranean. 'No nations seem wealthier', wrote Alexandrian geographer Agatharchides in about 110 B.C., 'than the Sabaeans and the Gerrhaeans, who are the agents of everything that falls under the name of transport from Asia to Europe.'

To prevent their customers from trading direct and thus maintain their lucrative monopoly of Eastern trade, Arabian intermediaries jealously kept secret their sources of supply, so that for centuries the Greeks and Romans believed that the kingdoms of southwest Arabia produced all the luxuries of the Orient. Hence Rome's description of this region as *Arabia Felix* – fortunate Arabia.

Arabia's fortune, however, made others envious. Alexander the Great planned to invade the Arabian Peninsula and seize its riches but death, in 323 B.C., forestalled him. Alexander's successors, the Ptolemies, sought to bypass Arabia: sailing from southern Egypt down the Red Sea to Eudaemon, on the southern shores of Arabia, in about 200 B.C. in search of oriental merchandise. They then pushed farther east along Arabia's southern shores until, in 116 B.C., like the Europeans centuries later, they learnt the secret of riding the monsoon winds across the open seas to India.

In spite of the Ptolemies' activities, however, trade between Egypt and India remained largely in Arab hands, for although the old channels of trade were paralleled, they were not conquered. So strong were the age-old contacts between Arabs and Indians that the Arabs

continued to dominate the spice trade – cinnamon, for example, still being kept secret from Western merchants even in Indian ports.

It was to break Arab control of Eastern trade that the Roman Emperor Augustus – having made Egypt part of the Roman Empire – sent an expedition against the Sabaeans of southwest Arabia in 24 B.C. But the Roman army crossed the Red Sea too far north and had to march hundreds of miles along Arabia's arid western coast, so that on arrival in the south the soldiers were too weak and reduced in numbers for action and had to withdraw.

Defeated by the desert, the Romans now sought to bypass Arabia and its intermediaries' mark-ups and transit tolls; expanding the direct sea route between Egypt and India, inaugurated by the Greeks, by diverting traffic through the Red Sea to the port of Myos Hormos, overland to Coptus and up the Nile to Alexandria.

Although today the exact location of Myos Hormos is not sure, it is likely that it stood in the region of present-day al-Qusayr, at the Red Sea end of the road we took through the Wadi Hammamat from Qus. Once the most important Egyptian port on the Red Sea, al-Qusayr served the city of Qus, which in medieval Islamic Egypt was second only to Cairo in size and importance. Here Arab merchant ships unloaded their rich Eastern cargoes, and African Muslims set out for, and returned from, the pilgrimage to Makkah.

After a period of decline al-Qusayr was revived by Egypt's Ottoman rulers, but following the opening of the Suez Canal in the nineteenth century the old port fell into disuse. Today sandpipers strut undisturbed along its near-deserted shore, and a pile of Ottoman cannon lie rusting beside its unattended, one-room customs post.

THE SAUDI SEAPORT OF JIDDAH STILL PRESERVES IN THE HOMES OF FORMER MERCHANTS THE ANCIENT TRADING ATMOSPHERE ON THE RED SEA.

Ships leaving Myos Hormos for India in ancient times held their course down the middle of the Red Sea as far as Muza – modern Mocha, in present-day Yemen. This, according to *The Periplus of the Erythraean Sea*, a first-century B.C. shipping guide written by an unknown Greek merchant from Egypt, was because the Red Sea shores of what is now Saudi Arabia were 'terrible in every way'.

'Navigation', the *Periplus* warned, 'is dangerous along this whole coast, which is without harbours, with bad anchorages, foul, inaccessible because of breakers and rocks.' Today, by contrast, the Red Sea coast of Saudi Arabia boasts some of the most sophisticated ports in the Near East, including Jiddah, Jizan and the giant oil and gas terminal of Yanbu. The Red Sea can still, however, be treacherous; a fact dramatically brought home to us while we were in Egypt by the sinking in a storm of the regular ferry boat from Suez to Jiddah, with the loss of many lives.

Formerly a quiet seaport under Ottoman suzerainty with a population of 30,000 living within an area of a few square kilometres, Jiddah is now a mega-metropolis and ultra-modern seaport. Today it has a population of over 1.5 million spread over some 400 square kilometres (154 square miles). Although old fishing boats mounted on concrete pedestals celebrate Jiddah's historic ties with the sea, its skyline is dominated by a futuristic navigational tower controlling shipping from around the globe.

A BRIGHTLY-LIT CEREMONIAL TENT REFLECTS ALEXANDRIA'S GLITTERING PAST AS A CROSSROADS OF COMMERCE FROM AFRICA, ASIA AND EUROPE.

Although the Arabs maintained a wide-ranging international caravan network for the greater part of the first millennium B.C., this system of overland trade was dealt a withering blow when the Romans began to process Indian and Far Eastern trade through Egypt, thus undermining the route through Arabia. Although overland routes played an important part in the early spice trade, it was by sea that the Arabs' involvement in the international spice trade later grew.

The *Periplus's* description of Muza confirms that Arab traders were already sailing from there to India and East Africa 2,000 years ago: 'And the whole place is crowded with Arab shipowners and seafaring men, and is busy with the affairs of commerce; for they carry on trade with the far-side coast [East Africa] and with Barygaza [in northwest India] sending their own ships there.'

Leaving the Red Sea through the strait of Bab al-Mandab, the Gate of Tears, the first port of call on Arabia's southern coast in earliest times was Eudaemon, present-day Aden. An ancient emporium of Arabia, its fortunes plummeted – probably after being sacked by rivals – so that by the first century, according to the *Periplus*, it was just 'a village by the shore'.

Eudaemon's fortunes did not revive until the Islamic era. Later during the age of steam, Aden became an important coaling station for ships en route from Europe to the Far East. Today it is the commercial capital of Yemen.

Continuing along the southern coast of Arabia, first century B.C. traders would have stopped off at Cana, near Mukalla in modern Yemen, to take on water before striking out across open seas to the Malabar ports of southwest India. Alternatively if their destination was northwest India they hugged the shore of Arabia to its eastern extremity, before crossing the Gulf of Oman and following the coast of what is now Iran and Pakistan to the mouth of the Indus River.

A regular port of call for coast-hugging craft was Moscha, also known as Sumhuram, situated just east of the modern-day city of Salalah, in Oman. According to the *Periplus*, 'Ships from Cana call here regularly, and ships returning from Barygaza, if the season is late, winter here and trade with the king's officers, trading their cloth and wheat and sesame oil for frankincense, which lies in heaps all over the country.'

Sumhuram was built by King Il'ad Yalut in the first century B.C. specifically for the export of frankincense. Potsherds and a bronze figurine from India, excavated there, attest to its once prosperous connection with both East and West. Today, however, it is but a ghostly ruin, perched on a hilltop overlooking a creek no longer connected to the sea. Although frankincense is still collected and sold nearby, it is only in small quantities and at a fraction of its former price. Thus, for only a few dollars in Salalah's market square, I was able to buy several kilos of frankincense – once worth its weight in gold.

Greco-Roman commerce with India reached its peak during the reigns of the Julio-Claudian and Flavian emperors, A.D. 31–96, when, according to Strabo, no fewer than 120 ships sailed in a single year from Egypt to India. Previously there had been only twenty. Under the emperors Trajan, Hadrian and the Antonines, from A.D. 98–192, maritime trade between India and the Roman Empire continued to flourish as ships with a carrying capacity of up to 500 tons beat with the monsoon winds between Egypt and Indian ports: Barbaricum at the mouth of the Indus, Barygaza further south, and Muziris, now Cranganore, 200 miles north of the southern tip of India, where they picked up not only goods from India, but also merchandise brought there from China and South-East Asia.

By A.D. 150, however, the Ethiopian kingdom of Aksum was challenging Rome's monopoly of Eastern trade by way of the Red Sea, and finally, during the third century, with the economic decline of the Roman Empire – partly because of its imbalance of trade with the East – Greco-Roman traffic in the Indian Ocean withered away. The demand for Oriental goods did not, however, vanish. The eastern provinces of the Roman Empire remained prosperous under the Byzantines, whose capital Constantinople, now Istanbul, replaced Rome as the most prestigious city in Europe and the emporium of the Christian world.

In Persia, meanwhile, the Sassanian revolution had brought to power a dynamic new leadership, which conquered every passage to the East, including the sea lanes of the Indian Ocean. With control of the overland Silk Roads across Persia as well as the maritime Spice Route in their hands, the Sassanids regained for the Near East the monopoly of Asian trade lost briefly to Europe – a supremacy over the land and sea routes linking East and West that was not only reinforced but also expanded by the advent of Islam.

A FORT BUILT BY THE PORTUGUESE STANDS GUARD OVER MUSCAT. THE HARBOUR WAS SEIZED BY THE PORTUGUESE IN 1507 AS A BASE TO EXPAND INTO THE INDIAN OCEAN.

THE ARABIAN SEA

A MEDIEVAL GLASS PAINTING OF A TRADITIONAL ARAB DHOW.

The start of the second stage of our journey along the Spice Route was far more fitting than the first: a pipe and drum band played a stirring farewell as Oman's royal yacht, the *Fulk al-Salamah*, set sail from Muscat for the Far East. The luxury cruiser had been loaned by Sultan Qaboos to UNESCO to retrace – like us – ancient trade routes. We were to travel intermittently aboard her.

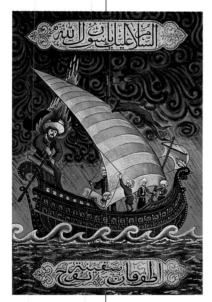

UNESCO's purpose in retracing these routes – it had already sent similar expeditions along the overland Silk Roads – was to highlight their historical role as a means of communication. The merchant mariners who travelled the Spice Route carried with them not only their wares, but their customs, cultures and religions too.

For example Indians, who were the primary carriers of early Eastern sea trade, spread Hinduism to all parts of South-East Asia, where as a result largely autonomous Indianized states emerged on the Malay Peninsula and Indonesian archipelago in the first century A.D. Many of the 24 per cent Christian population of the modern Indian state of Kerala trace their beliefs to Syrian Orthodox spice traders who settled on the subcontinent's southwest Malabar coast in A.D. 345.

The most far-reaching and long-lasting change, however, was that effected by Muslim merchants and missionaries in the Middle Ages. They spread the teachings of the Prophet Muhammad along the Spice Route from Arabia to Pakistan, the Maldive Islands, Malaya, Brunei and Indonesia, which remain Muslim states to this day, as well as India, Sri Lanka, Thailand, the Philippines and China, where Islam is still widespread.

The world-altering rise of Islam in the seventh century radically changed patterns of international trade too. Within a quarter of a century of unifying the pagan tribes of Arabia through the monotheistic religion revealed to him, Muhammad and his successors – the caliphs – had conquered most lands at the western end of the Spice Route, including Egypt, Mesopotamia, Syria, Palestine and Persia. Two rival faiths now confronted each other across the Mediterranean, which instead of a highway became a frontier. The Red Sea and Arabian Gulf were no longer rival routes to Europe and Persia, but parallel ones to the unified lands of Islam.

By the ninth century, Baghdad had become a vast centre of population and wealth, the commercial metropolis of the Middle East and capital of an Islamic empire stretching from the Atlantic to the borders of China and India. Luxury goods arrived regularly from the East, by caravan across Central Asia – now also under Arab rule – and aboard ships of the empire, which made regular voyages down the Arabian Gulf and across the Indian Ocean to South-East Asia and China, even pushing further east along the Indonesian archipelago for the lucrative spice trade, previously in the hands of the Malays.

Arabs established trading colonies in India, Sri Lanka, Malaysia and Indonesia, and developed an Asian-wide trading system with Muslim merchants at its axis. Arab ships

A REPLICA OF AN OCEAN-GOING ARAB DHOW BUILT IN OMAN AND SAILED TO SINGAPORE TO COMMEMORATE EARLY TRADING VOYAGES BY ARAB MARINERS TO SOUTH-EAST ASIA.

traded routinely from one end of the Spice Route to the other, and the Arabian *dinar* replaced the Persian *dirham* as the standard currency of East–West trade.

The main western terminus of the Spice Route was now al-Basra, a new port founded by the Arabs at the head of the Gulf, from where goods were shipped by river craft up the Tigris and Euphrates to Baghdad. If bound for Europe they were then caravanned across the Syrian desert to Antioch, in modern Turkey, which replaced Alexandria as the main entrepôt for the Mediterranean.

The Sultanate of Oman – at the mouth of the Gulf and on the edge of the Arabian Sea – played a special role in this trade; ships waited in its ports for the monsoon winds to carry them across the Indian Ocean. As I saw en route to join the *Fulk al-Salamah*, Oman still serves a similar purpose: many tankers were anchored off its northern shore waiting their turn to enter the Gulf to collect oil cargoes.

We were travelling to Muscat from Suhar, a port town to the north, which is the legendary home of Sinbad the Sailor. Oman not only served as an anteroom to the Gulf, it also built its ships with teak brought there from India, provisioned them for their long ocean voyage with food and water from its fertile shores, and finally provided most of their crews.

Suhar also exported copper extracted from mines nearby. It was from these mines, archaeologists believe, that the Sumerians of Mesopotamia obtained the copper on which their civilization – the forerunner of our own – was based.

Suhar was a centre of Sassanian maritime activity from the third century A.D., but reached its peak in Muslim times when, according to Arab historian al-Maqadisi, it was 'the hallway to China, the store house of the East and Iraq, and the mainstay of Yemen'. Al-Maqadisi, who sailed from Suhar with Arab merchants, said its anchorage was 4 miles (6.5 kilometres) long and busy with ships, while the town itself had 12,000 houses – each captain his own residence – and a great mosque near the shore with a tall minaret and a magnificent, many-coloured *mihrab*.

Although it is hard for the modern visitor to imagine Suhar's past glories, some reminders do remain: the dazzling white coastal garrison, originally built by the Sassanians, has been restored to its original splendour; a great modern mosque – also with tall minaret and magnificent *mihrab* – has been built by the shore; and copper is again being extracted and exported from Suhar's recently reopened mines to world markets.

Oman has had contact with the outside world by sea since earliest times: seals excavated at Maysar, in central Oman, indicate contact with India as early as the third millennium B.C. Certainly, by the beginning of the second millennium ships were sailing from there along the southern coasts of what is now Iran and Pakistan to harbours at the mouth of the Indus River.

It was this ancient coast-hugging route that our modern mini-cruise ship now followed, although with a weight of 10,864 tons and a length of 130 metres (420 feet), with four engines giving a maximum speed of 19.5 knots, a flight deck and hanger for two helicopters and garages for twelve limousines, the *Fulk al-Salamah* was a far cry from the traditional Arab dhow whose course we took.

The dhow's chief characteristics were neither size nor luxury, but the manner in which the wooden planks of the hull were sewn, not nailed, together, and the fore and

THE RESTORED FORT AT SOHAR, LEGENDARY BIRTHPLACE OF SINBAD THE SAILOR, ON ARABIA'S SOUTHERN COAST.

aft set of the sails. This so-called 'lateen' rig allowed the yardarm to swing freely and the sail to billow out when the ship was running before the wind, while the rope-sewn planks gave the vessel great resilience.

As the indefatigable Arab traveller Ibn Battuta wrote in the *Rihlah* – an account of his journeys across Africa, Asia and the Indian Ocean, 'If a ship nailed together with iron collides with rocks it would surely be wrecked; but a ship whose beams are sewn together with rope is not shattered.' The fourteenth-century Muslim judge was writing from bitter experience, for only piety saved him from drowning when his junk was likewise wrecked; he was ashore at the time attending Friday noon prayers. Motorized dhows still ply the coastal waters of the Arabian Sea, but, as I saw in a Karachi boatyard, unlike their forbearers their planks are now nailed – not sewn – together.

Our reception in – as well as voyage to – Karachi was in sharp contrast too to that of earlier travelers. Instead of pirates, for which the Indus estuary was once notorious, we were besieged by scores of flag-bedecked fishing boats full of dancers and musicians, who escorted us noisily up river to a warm welcome at Port Bin Qasim – appropriately named after the teenage Arab general, who in 711 suppressed the Indus Delta pirates The 17-year-old Muhhamad ibn al-Qasim's conquest of the lower Indus Valley – now the Pakistani province of Sind – also gave the Arabs the strategic port of Debal at the mouth of the Indus River, and brought them a stage nearer to the Far East and eventual domination of maritime spice trade.

As archaeologists have identified ancient ruins 64 kilometres (40 miles) inland from Karachi as the site of Debal, Wheeler and I left the *Fulk al-Salamah* to continue its journey by sea, while we continued ours by road. Debal, or as the ancients called it Barbaricum, once stood according to the *Periplus* on one of the seven mouths of the Indus River, and was for more than a millennium the main entrepôt of Sind. Centuries of silting and occasional earthquakes have altered the course of the Indus and driven back the sea, so that Debal today stands derelict on the shore of an obscure creek. Impressive remains of eighth-century walls, built of limestone blocks, with

A WARM WELCOME FROM PAKISTANI FISHERMEN TO THE INDUS ESTUARY CONTRASTS SHARPLY TO THAT OF PIRATES WHO ONCE PREYED ON RICH SPICE ROUTE TRADE.

semicircular bastions at regular intervals, do however give the modern visitor some idea of the port city's size and importance. Pottery and coins displayed in a museum nearby indicate that it once traded with Muslim territories to the west, and with countries as far east as China.

East of the Indus estuary, at what the *Periplus* describes as 'the beginning of all India', lies the Gulf of Gujarat, a name once synonymous with East–West maritime trade. Its ports drew foreign merchants from earliest times, while its own traders founded mercantile colonies as far away as Indonesia, and created a commercial network that lasted in the Indian Ocean until the sixteenth-century conquests of the Portuguese.

Excavated remains of a port city at Lothal, on the Gulf of Gujarat's western shores, date back as far as the second millennium B.C., when it is believed to have traded with ancient Egypt and Mesopotamia. Barygaza, on the gulf's eastern shore, flourished in classical times, and Cambay, at the head of the gulf, was one of the greatest emporiums of the Muslim era.

Little is known of Lothal, but detailed descriptions of Barygaza and Cambay do remain. According to the *Periplus*, access to Barygaza was 'very dangerous. For the rush of waters at incoming tide is irresistible, so that large ships are caught up by its force,

turned broadside on through the speed of the current, and driven on the shoals and wrecked.'

There were rich rewards, however, for merchant mariners who braved these hazards. As well as ivory and spices such as spikenard and pepper, according to the *Periplus* Barygaza also traded in 'great quantities' of the precious stones agate and carnelian, and 'all kinds of muslins and mallow cloth' from both northern and peninsular India. These goods were carried by 'wagons through great tracts of land without roads', while from the north 'raw silk, silk yarn and silk cloth' were brought from Bactria, in Central Asia, on foot. Imports included 'wine, Italian preferred, bright girdles a cubit in width....

And for the King costly vessels of silver, singing boys [and] beautiful maidens for the harem.'

When Ibn Battuta visited Gujarat in the thirteenth century, Barygaza had been eclipsed by Cambay, the majority of whose inhabitants, he wrote in the *Rihlah*, were 'foreign merchants, who continually build beautiful houses and wonderful mosques – an achievement in which they endeavour to surpass each other.' Many of these merchants were Arabs or Persians migrating in and out of Cambay with the rhythm of the monsoons, but others were Muslims whose families had settled in the town generations, even centuries, earlier, intermarrying with Gujarati women and assimilating everyday customs of the Hindu hinterland.

The conquest of Gujarat by the Sultans of Delhi in 1297 further strengthened the position of its Muslim merchants, who by then were not only sailing as far as South-East Asia in search of silk and spices, but were also establishing themselves as commercial partners and political allies of local rulers of lands all along the Spice Route.

Meanwhile, in Central Asia in the thirteenth century, Genghis Khan united the Mongols, destroyed the caravan cities of Bukhara, Samarkand, Tashkent, Balkh and Marv, and extinguished the Abbasid caliphate in Baghdad. Paradoxically one of the results of this bloody eruption from the steppes was closer links between East and West. The Mongols ruled from the Mediterranean to the Pacific, and controlled the Silk Roads through Central Asia. For the first time merchants from Europe – Marco Polo among them – were able to travel safely under Mongol protection to China. During this so-called 'Mongol peace', which lasted more than a century, Europe and China came into direct contact for the first time.

This reopening of the way for overland trade came too late, however, to change the shift in favour of the maritime routes. Although sea voyages were still open to attacks by pirates, the risk of storm and the threat of scurvy, they were not as hazardous as the land journey. Above all, for the merchants who sponsored them, they avoided the tolls and the intermediaries' commissions that would have been exacted in Central Asia.

Although the main overland trade routes across Central Asia withered and died, many others flourished, especially those linking inland population centres with Spice Route ports. One such route was the caravan trail north from the Gulf of Gujarat to the upper Indus and Ganges valleys. Straddling this route, on the edge of the Thar Desert in present-day Rajasthan, lay the fortress city of Jaisalmer.

As it is one of the few medieval citadels still inhabited today, we detoured there on a one-vehicle-wide ribbon of asphalt. Our driver played what at first appeared to be 'chicken' with vehicles coming head-on, but it transpired to be simply good Indian road manners, each driver giving up half the asphalt to the other at the very last moment without even slowing down.

The unnerving drive was however worthwhile. Suddenly out of the dusty plain rose a mighty hill dominated by an awesome citadel, its yellow sandstone ramparts tinged golden by the setting sun. Built by a Rajput prince in 1156, Jaisalmer's position astride the overland subsidiary of the Spice Route brought it great wealth, and its merchants built magnificent mansions with exquisitely carved facades of wood and stone. These still stand today outside the city walls where laden caravans once halted, while within the citadel's encircling bastions three elaborate medieval Jain temples and 800 houses are still in use.

Today a living museum, Jaisalmer was sidetracked in the eighteenth century by the rise of Bombay – which is now, by contrast, the powerhouse of India. Bombay is the nation's richest and fastest-moving city, home of its biggest banking institutions, and its busiest sea port, handling nearly half of India's foreign trade.

Landing at the Gateway to India – Bombay's welcoming waterfront landmark – it was hard to image this teeming city as it once was: a group of malarial mudflats given to the British by their Portuguese occupiers in 1661 as part of Catherine of Braganza's dowry in marriage to Charles II. He leased them for the princely sum of £10 per annum to the fledgling British East India Company, which made Bombay its trading headquarters for the whole west coast of India, triggering the meteoric expansion that still continues there today.

Ibn Battuta, when he passed this way, counted twelve thriving trading states strung out along India's western coast from Gujarat in the north to Cape Comorin at its southern tip. Although these maritime kingdoms were Hindu, the culture of their ports was a long-simmering synthesis of Islamic law and practice with local Hindu customs, styles, dress and cuisine, while their governments were nothing less than a working partnership between the rajas, whose wealth was almost entirely dependent on customs revenues, and the leading Muslim merchants who lived there.

An exception to this Indo-Islamic alliance was Gowapur, a port on the River Mandovi estuary 400 kilometres (250 miles) south of Bombay, over which Muslims and Hindus fought each other for centuries. Gowapur dominated the trade of the legendary wealthy Vijayanagar Hindu empire of peninsular India, and was an important landing place for Arabian horses for its cavalry. As such, it was a favourite target for Vijayanagar's main rivals – the Muslim rulers of northern India, who, while leaving the smaller Hindu maritime states largely alone, regularly raided Gowapur and occupied it from the fourteenth to sixteenth centuries.

This rivalry gave the Portuguese, who were successfully resisted elsewhere by strong Hindu–Muslim alliances, their first foothold in the Indian Ocean. When Alfonso de Albuquerque's armada of twenty-three ships and 1,000 men sailed into the Arabian Sea in 1509, the commander of Vijayanagar's navy implored him to attack Gowapur, then in the hands of the Muslim Adil Shahis. This he did, seizing the port – not for Vijayanagar but for Portugal, which renamed it Goa and made it capital of its fledgling Asian trading empire.

GOA'S LATIN LANGUOR AND FINE BEACHES MAKE IT ONE OF INDIA'S MOST POPULAR TOURIST DESTINATIONS.

Portugal held the Goa enclave until 1961, endowing it with an Iberian legacy still clearly visible today: whitewashed churches with twin towers dot its lush green landscape, while old houses with overhanging balconies and red-tiled roofs line the streets of its towns. Goa's Latin languor and fine beaches make it one of India's most popular tourist destinations, enabling us to spend our nights there in a five-star beach-front hotel, while visiting magnificent medieval churches by day.

South of Goa, stretching along India's southwest seaboard, lie the Malabar coast ports of Calicut, Cranganore, Cochin and Quilon, where – at different times – the Greeks and Romans, Arabs and Chinese, Syrian Christians and Jews, Portuguese, British and Dutch established trading colonies. All these foreign merchants came to modern-day Kerala for the same reason: black pepper, grown on the lush slopes of the Western Ghats highlands, which run parallel to the Malabar coast, trapping the rain-laden monsoon winds.

The Western Ghats are ideal for the pepper plant, which for best growth requires a long rainy season, not too high temperatures and partial shade, the latter being provided by interspersing the pepper vine among the tea plantations which cover the Western Ghats. Propagation is by stem cuttings, which are set out near a tree or pole that will serve as support for the woody climber, which may reach heights of 10 metres (33 feet) by means of its aerial roots. The vine starts bearing berries – or peppercorns – in two to five years, and under good conditions my produce for as long as forty years.

Pepper – long one of the most prized spices known – has been grown on the Malabar coast since ancient times. Classical Tamil poetry tells that, for example,

CHINESE FISHING NETS LINE THE BAY OF COCHIN, MODERN-DAY CENTRE OF MALABAR'S SPICE TRADE.

> *the beautiful large ships of the Yavans*
> *[Greco-Roman merchants] bringing gold,*
> *come splashing the white foam on the waters . . . and return laden with pepper.*

Not only was Malabar a spice producer in its own right, it was also the hinge on which turned all the maritime trade of the Indian Ocean. The Spice Route was not simply a single sea lane, but a series of routes feeding in from east and west to India at the centre. From the west, routes ran down either side of the Arabian Peninsula and from the east coast of Africa across the Arabian Sea to southern India, while from the east, routes ran from China and Indonesia across the Bay of Bengal to also converge at southern India.

The Malabar coast served as transit centre for trade between the two halves of the Indian Ocean, and Cranganore was its major port for nearly a millennium. The *Periplus* said Muziris, as Cranganore was known in the first antiquity, 'abounds in ships sent there with Arabian cargoes, and by the Greeks'. The remains of a temple dedicated to Roman Emperor Augustus are evidence that a fair number of Greek and Roman merchants lived there in the first century B.C.

Tradition has it too that both Christianity and Islam entered India through Cranganore. St. Thomas is said to have established India's first church there in A.D. 52, while 600 years later, a party of learned Muslims landed there and built India's first mosque.

Records left behind by Arab mariners indicate Cranganore was eclipsed in the ninth and tenth centuries as southern India's chief entrepôt by Quilon, gateway to a maze of inland backwaters used to carry the rich produce of Kerala's interior to the coast. The idea of using these backwaters as a quick transport system is credited to the Muslim ruler

THE BACKWATERS OF INDIA'S MALABAR COAST ARE STILL USED AS TRANSPORT BETWEEN INLAND SETTLEMENTS AND COASTAL PORTS.

Tipu Sultan, but it was the British who perfected this canal system, which still functions today.

By the time Vasco da Gama landed at Calicut in 1498 – to become the first European to reach India via the sea route around the southern cape of Africa – it was the new Hindu power centre of Malabar, with Muslim merchants in charge of its trade.

Portugal's first attempts to conquer Calicut, in 1509 and 1510, were repulsed by an alliance of its Hindu ruler, the Zamorin or Lord of the Sea, and his Muslim-led navy, the Marakars. And although the Zamorin was finally forced to capitulate – for only by extinguishing such Hindu–Muslim strongholds could Portugal control the spice trade – the legend of the Marakars lingers on in the songs that the Malabar fishers sing as they put out to sea.

The Chinese too had a base near Calicut: a fort called 'Chinna-kotah', for it was at Malabar that the commercial domains of the Chinese junk and the Arab dhow met. The normal pattern – at least until the Portuguese developed direct links with the Orient – was for lateen-rigged dhows to carry goods across the western half on the Indian Ocean, and lug-type fore and aft sail junks to carry them across the eastern half.

Arab merchants endowed Calicut with a lasting Islamic character, best evidenced today by its Muchunthi Palli, whose architecture combines the austere elegance of Islam with the exuberance of Kerala. But the Chinese left the most conspicuous trace in the daily life of Kerala: eye-catching cantilevered fishing nets, introduced by traders from the court of Kublai Khan, are strung out like great butterfly wings along its coconut palm-fringed coast and languid backwaters. These are at their most spectacular silhouetted against the evening sky at Cochin, their nets held high as if to catch the setting sun.

Cochin is the present-day centre of Malabar's spice trade. In its quaint old quarter of Mattancherry, scores of small firms huddle together in dilapidated old buildings filled with the pungent aroma of pepper, ginger and cardamom. In some buildings men manhandled large sacks of ginger root-stems amidst stinging dust, while in others women in colourful saris graded dark brown peppercorns, thousands of which were drying on the floor of adjoining courtyards or, packed in sacks, being loaded on to trucks for transportation to Cochin's modern sea port to be loaded on freighters for shipment – as in the past – to overseas markets. The main customers for India's annual 45,000-ton pepper exports today are Russia and the United States.

If any one building in Cochin best sums up the Spice Route's past, it is the oldest European-built church in India, standing testimony to historical developments in Malabar as first the Portuguese, then the Dutch, and finally the British seized control of the spice trade. Built in 1503 by Franciscan friars, it became a Protestant church with the arrival of the Dutch in 1663, turned Anglican in 1795 with British occupation, and since independence has been run by the Church of South India. Such were the changing fortunes of the spice trade.

THE INDIAN OCEAN

We sailed into Male, capital of the Maldives archipelago, in a tropical storm so intense that it briefly forced the tiny craft in which we were now travelling to hove to into the wind for fear of being swamped. It was a dramatic reminder of just one of the many hazards faced by Spice Route traders; scurvy and pirates at sea, dust storms, thirst and brigands on land, being others among them. But the seemingly solid wall of rain, accompanied by lightening and thunder, passed as quickly as it came, leaving us wet, cold and bedraggled, but soon warmed and dried by the Equatorial sun.

OCEAN-GOING ARAB DHOWS ONCE STOPPED OFF AT INDIAN OCEAN ISLANDS AS THEY RODE THE MONSOONS ACROSS THE ARABIAN SEA, BUT TODAY ONLY FISHING BOATS PLY THEIR WATERS.

Drizzled across the Equator like a string of pearls, some 720 kilometres (450 miles) off the southern tip of India, the Maldives Islands were the first stop-off on an island-hopping tour of the Indian Ocean, which made up the third stage of our journey retracing the Spice Route. Although they are now something of a backwater, these 1,196 palm-tree-covered coral-reef-ringed islands once provided regular anchorage for ocean-going dhows engaged in international trade.

The Maldivians have been trading and fishing folks since earliest times, for not only were their islands strategically located along the old Indian Ocean trading routes, but they also produced two commodities vital to East–West commerce. One was coir, or coconut fibre, used to stitch together the hulls of dhows. The other was the shells of the little marine gastropod called the cowrie, which were once used as currency as far east as Malaysia and as far west as the African Sudan.

Fishing remains the mainstay of the island's economy, and I spent a fascinating day fishing for tuna. As I watched, the fishermen first netted thousands of tiny fish in the shallows, then sailed out to sea with the fish swimming around in their partly water-filled craft. On sighting a tuna shoal they began frantically ladling their live bait into the sea, and as the hungry tuna rushed in to feed they deftly hauled them aboard with a baitless hook and line.

Apart from some shuttle trade between Malabar and the Maldives, the islands today are bypassed by international commerce. Essentially a place for diving enthusiasts and for lazing in the sun, their 'desert island' look does, however, attract tourists from all over the world. This could change: averaging in size only 4 square kilometres (1.5 square miles), and in no place no more than a couple of metres above sea level, scientists fear rising sea levels, caused by global warming, could one day cause this lost paradise to disappear altogether.

From the Maldive atolls eastbound traders headed for Sri Lanka, where Adam's Peak was the landfall they looked for. It got its name from the belief that when Adam was cast down from Paradise this was where his foot first touched Earth. 'Our sailors can see the peak where Adam fell from nine days off,' wrote a ninth-century Arab chronicler, 'and they steer towards it.'

Arab traders gave the island the name Sarandib; the Portuguese called it Ceilao, which the Dutch altered to Ceylan and the British to Ceylon. In 1972 the island was officially

renamed Lanka – by which it had always been known to its majority Sinhalese population – with the addition of Sri, meaning auspicious or resplendent.

Horace Walpole, in a fairy tale called The *Three Princes of Serendip*, expanded the Arab name Sarandib into serendipity, or what the dictionary now calls 'an aptitude for making desirable discoveries by accident'. For us too our stopover in Sri Lanka was one of unexpectedly pleasant surprises.

Shaped like a teardrop falling from India, Sri Lanka once served as a trans-shipment centre for goods moving between the two halves of the Indian Ocean. It was also an important source of cinnamon and precious stones. The island and its valuable products have long been known in international trade. Historians believe that it may have been the Tarshish of Biblical times, where King Solomon obtained gems, spices and peacocks, while the *Periplus* refers to it as Palaesidmundu, famous for 'pearls, transparent stones and tortoiseshell'.

The Romans, in their attempts to circumvent the Arab monopoly of East–West trade, turned to Sri Lanka for intercepting supplies of silks and spices from South-East Asia. After the Sassanians came to power in Persia in A.D. 222, it became an important junction where they and the Romans jostled each other to trade with the Chinese. By the sixth century the island had become a major trading center to which, according to Cosmas Indicopleustes of Alexandria, came the 'richest merchandise of the Indies, and all sorts of spices and perfumes'.

PREVIOUS SPREAD KECHEMALAI MOSQUE AT BERUWELD MARKS THE LOCATION OF THE FIRST RECORDED SETTLEMENT OF MUSLIM MERCHANTS ON SRI LANKA IN 1024.

By the eighth century there had grown up on Sri Lanka an Arab–Muslim trading community, who maintained a supply agency for their principals in south Indian ports. The Arab traders established themselves at strategic points on the island's western coast, from where they were able to penetrate the interior to get at the source of gems in the vicinity of Adam's Peak. The story of Sinbad the Sailor's adventures in the Valley of Diamonds, which represents a kernel of true history in a romantic setting, bears testimony to the close relations between Sri Lanka and the Caliphate of Baghdad.

So too do recent archaeological discoveries 112 kilometres (70 miles) east of the Sri Lankan capital of Colombo, where workings have revealed hundreds of extraordinary monsoon-powered furnaces, believed to have produced the toughened iron used to make the weapons that helped created the Islamic empire.

It was cinnamon, however, that drew the Dutch to Sri Lanka, where they began intensive cultivation of the native laurel *Cinnamomum zeylanicum* in the eighteenth century. Even today the best-quality cinnamon is said to come from Sri Lanka, harvested in May and June when the bark from which the spice is obtained is full of sap. Shoots are first scraped with a semicircular blade, then rubbed with a brass rod to loosen the bark, which is split with a knife and peeled. The peels are telescoped into one another, forming a quill about 107 centimetres (42 inches) long, and filled with trimmings of the same quality bark to maintain the cylindrical shape. After four or five days' drying, the quills are rolled on a board to tighten the filling, then placed in subdued sunlight for further drying.

For the Dutch, the most important source of cinnamon was Negombo on Sri Lanka's western coast, and we found many reminders there of the days when they ruled the island. It was here, for example, that the Dutch revealed more than anywhere else in Asia their love of canals, which still run north–south through Negombo, a total distance of over 120 kilometres (75 miles), and a stolid Dutch fort still stands close to the lagoon around which Negombo is built.

THE LAGOON AROUND WHICH NEGOMBO – ONCE THE WORLD'S MAIN SOURCE OF CINNAMON – IS BUILT.

The port's most colorful link with the past, however, is indigenous: its fishermen – like their forbearers for centuries before them – sweeping back into the lagoon in their outrigger sail boats each afternoon, to land and auction off their catch amidst boisterous bargaining.

Sri Lanka's most historically interesting town, however, is Galle. Sea-going ships trading eastbound from the Arabian Sea or westbound from the Bay of Bengal could not sail through the straits that divided Sri Lanka from the Indian subcontinent, because of the extremely shallow reef called Adam's Bridge that blocked the channel. They had to go instead around the southern tip of Sri Lanka, and it was here that Galle grew up.

After the Portuguese seized control of the spice trade they built a small fort here in 1598, which they later extended with a series of walls and bastions. Following their takeover of the island in 1640, the Dutch built the 36 hectare (90 acre) fort, which stands in almost perfect repair today, and encompasses all the older part of Galle. By the time Sri Lanka passed into British hands, commercial interest was turning to Colombo, and Galle has scarcely altered since the Dutch left. It is a delightful little place, quiet and easy-going within the old fort walls, and with a real sense of being steeped in history.

Galle's original gate bears witness to the port's changing fortunes. It is topped on the outer side by the British coat of arms, while inside the letters VOC are inscribed in the stone. They stand for the Dutch *Vereenigde Oost-Indische Compagnie*, or Dutch East India Company, and are flanked by two lions and topped by a cock. The VOC was a landmark in the history of capitalism. One of the first global corporations, it was formed in 1602 to pool the resources of several Netherlands ports for the purpose of displacing Portugal in the spice trade. In Asia it was also a state in its own right, minting money, fighting wars and concluding treaties.

Arab traders too have left their mark in Galle, evidenced by several mosques and an Arabic College established in 1892, but like the island itself, the exotic-sounding Street of the Moorish Traders has been renamed. It is now simply New Street.

THE PROTESTANT CHURCH BUILT BY DUTCH COLONISTS AT MALACCA IS STILL IN USE TODAY.

We had intended to rejoin the *Fulk al-Salamah* at Madras for her voyage across the Bay of Bengal, but dawdling and detours had delayed us so much that we resorted instead to speedier transport: jetting across the eastern half of the Indian Ocean – a journey that would have taken early Spice Route traders months of hazardous sailing – in just a few hours.

Our destination was the Malacca Strait, the strategic link in the trade between India and China, connecting the Bay of Bengal with the South China Sea between the Malay peninsula and the island of Sumatra. Like the Malabar coast of southern India, the strait was a hinge in the monsoon sailing system, for vessels crossing the Bay of Bengal eastbound on the summer monsoon could not normally reach China or the Spice Islands before the opposing northeast wind set in, so Middle East merchants would winter in a port along the strait before continuing around the Malay peninsula and across the South China Sea in April or May. Indian-based merchants would sell their goods in the strait towns, then return directly to Malabar on the winter wind. Chinese ships followed the same seasonal pattern of travel, only in reverse.

Poised in the epicentre of the shifting monsoons, and located halfway down the strait on a mangrove-free river mouth, deep enough for ocean-going vessels, was the powerful port-city state of Malacca, from which the strait takes is name. Founded out of the chaos that convulsed South-East Asia at the end of the fourteenth century by Parameswara, a

fugitive prince from the declining Srivijaya empire of south Sumatra, Malacca became one of the most famous trading enclaves of the East.

By embracing Islam, Malacca strengthened its links with India and the Middle Eastern Muslim merchants who monopolized the spice trade in the Indian Ocean and who supplied, at exorbitant prices, the powerful states of the Mediterranean. By the middle of the fifteenth century it was the main entrepôt of South-East Asia and chief collecting point of spices from Indonesia.

According to Tome' Pires, a Portuguese accountant who lived in Malacca at the beginning of the sixteenth century, at least eighty-four distinct languages were spoken in its markets. Here too, wrote D.F.A.E. Koek in his *Portuguese History of Malacca*, were found 'cloves of Ternate, the nutmegs and mace of Banda, the sandalwood of Timor, the camphor of Borneo, curiosities of China, Japan and Siam'.

SMALL SAILING CRAFT HAVE REPLACED THE STATELY JUNKS, DHOWS AND GALLEONS WHICH ONCE PLIED THE INDIAN OCEAN.

Attracted by the vast profits to be made from trade in nutmeg and cloves, the Portuguese besieged Malacca in 1511, until it fell after seventeen days. Europe's first foothold in South-East Asia, Malacca was fought over by local sovereigns and rival foreign powers for the next 300 years. As the Portuguese writer Barebose put it, 'Whoever is Lord of Malacca has his hand on the throat of Venice' – Europe's main medieval entrepôt for Oriental trade.

The Portuguese turned Malacca into a mighty stronghold, whose walls withstood repeated attacks for 130 years. It finally fell in 1641, to the superior firepower of the Dutch, who after 150 years of occupation lost it in turn to the British.

For centuries a city of pivotal importance in global trade, Malacca is now just a cog in minor coastal commerce. Scruffy little motor sailors carrying wood and charcoal from neighbouring Sumatra have replaced the stately dhows, junks and galleons which brought gemstones, perfumes, silks and spices from far lands. But it remains an exuberant cultural mix, the Chinese, Arab, Javanese, Siamese, Indian, Portuguese, British and Dutch having all left their trace.

The old town square is dominated by the vermilion Protestant Christ Church, its original pews, used by Dutch colonizers at the inaugural services of 1753, still in use today. Nearby, the Stadhuys still stands massive and functional; having served uninterruptedly as the City Hall until 1980, it is now a magnificent museum.

The old city bustles beneath the stern gaze of the Spanish missionary Francis Xavier, whose statue still stands on a hilltop overlooking the harbour, while in the coastal suburb of Kampong Hiler descendants of Portuguese colonizers still speak the Iberian dialect, Cristao. Santiago Gate, however, is all that is little left of the formidable Portuguese walls that once surrounded old Malacca; the British dismantled them because they were too expensive to maintain. St. Paul's Church, originally built by Portuguese Captain Duarto Coelho in 1521 in gratitude for his escape from pirates in the South China Sea, is now just a shell; the Dutch converted it into a fort in 1753 and the British later used it as a powder store.

THE BRITISH COAT OF ARMS TOPS GALLE'S ORIGINAL GATEWAY, A REMINDER OF THE SPICE ROUTE PORT'S COLONIAL PAST.

Nowhere, however, is Malacca's colourful cosmopolitan past better illustrated than by the buildings on Temple Street. Here Kampong Keling Mosque with its typically Indonesian two-tier pyramidal roof and pagoda-like minaret stands between a shrine dedicated to the Hindu deity Vinayagar and a Chinese temple combing the doctrinal beliefs of Taoism, Confucianism and Buddhism. Such was the diversity of the Spice Route's Asian traders.

THE SPICE ISLANDS

THE SPICE ISLANDS

The final leg of our Spice Route odyssey took us from one end of the 13,677 island Indonesian archipelago to the other; from Sumatra, the second largest island in the world, to Rum, a mere speck on the edge of the Pacific Ocean, but one of major historical import. The Dutch, in their craving to control the Spice Islands, exchanged it with Britain – for nothing less than the island of Manhattan.

PEPPERCORNS (LEFT) AND NUTMEGS (BELOW) LAID OUT TO DRY IN THE SUN ARE STILL A COMMON SIGHT IN ANCIENT SPICE ROUTE PORTS.

NEXT SPREAD ALTHOUGH IT IS NO LONGER ONE OF THE WORLD'S MAIN SUPPLIERS, NUTMEG AND CLOVE TREES STILL FLOURISH ON THE SOIL-RICH VOLCANIC SLOPES OF TERNATE.

We began our journey at Aceh, Indonesia's westernmost province and the first landfall of eastbound Spice Route traders in South-East Asia. Involved in international trade since the ninth century, when Muslim merchants set up a forward base here for trade with the Orient, Aceh later became a major spice producer, expanding greatly the growing of pepper in Sumatra and shipping it directly to Egypt via Muslim ports in the Red Sea, to avoid Portuguese strongholds in India. By the 1550s, Aceh was supplying Europe with about half its pepper through this route, inevitably putting it on a collision course with European powers vying to monopolize the spice trade.

By the middle of the sixteenth century the Sultanate of Aceh was locked in a series of wars with the Portuguese colony of Malacca, in Malaysia. Aceh reached its zenith under the rule of Sultan Iskandar Muda (1607–36), when it briefly became one of the greatest powers in the region. Little remains of his opulent seventeenth-century capital, save a ghostly gateway of a vanished palace, destroyed by the Dutch when they invaded Aceh in 1853, and the ruins of the coastal fort where the Acehenese tried, but failed, to stop them.

Aceh underwent a new phase of independent commercial expansion from the 1780s, as private traders broke the fading monopolies of the Dutch and English East India companies. Private British and Tamil traders came from India, French pepper buyers from Mauritius and Reunion, and Americans from the maritime centres of New England. Captain Jonathan Carnes is credited with starting the US pepper trade with Sumatra, setting sail from Salem in the brigantine *Rajah* on 20 July 1795, and returning the following year with 158,544 tons of pepper, which sold at 37 cents per pound and brought a handsome profit of 700 per cent. This lucrative trade flourished for seventy years, with over 100 merchantmen laden with pepper entering Salem harbour alone, and many others sailing from Sumatra to Boston and New York.

American attention focused on the west coast of Sumatra between Sibolga and Meulaboh, where Acehenese river chiefs created the world's biggest centre of pepper production in the early decades of the nineteenth century. Our route, however, took us along the island's east coast to Medan, Sumatra's largest city and Indonesia's dominant port, handling a staggering 65 per cent of the nation's exports, including pepper, and enjoying a higher standard of living than any other Indonesian city.

The only true 'Indonesian' city, however, is Jakarta, Indonesia's dynamic capital, on the island of Java. Here is concentrated all the archipelago's human diversity: over 300 ethnic groups speaking more than 250

languages, in one major melting pot. Until 1527, when it was captured by Muslims, Jakarta was an entrepôt for the Hindu kingdom of Pajajaran, and known as Sunda Kelapa. This name and the atmosphere of the old Asian trading world are recalled today by Jakarta's Sunda Kelapa small ships harbour – where barefooted dockers bowed by heavy loads run up and down narrow bouncing gangplanks, unloading all manner of merchandise from brightly coloured Bugis schooners: tall, sleek, ketch-rigged craft which make up one of the world's major surviving sailing fleets.

In 1619 the Dutch East India Company made Jakarta the headquarters of the Netherlands' Asian trade. Restored seventeenth-century Dutch warehouses now serve as a maritime museum and – appropriately – a depository for spice trade memorabilia. It was here that the Dutch stored 1,500 tons of cloves in order to profit from the inevitable shortage in Europe following their destruction of all the clove trees on all but two islands they controlled.

Hundreds of thousands of cloves still go up in smoke each year in Indonesia – as cigarettes, consisting of some 50 per cent chopped cloves, mixed with tobacco, and sauced with lime and other tropical fruit juices, coconut sugar and perfume. Hand-rolling clove cigarettes – or 'kretek' – has been an art in Indonesia since the middle of the nineteenth century. At Kudus, in central Java, we watched the fleeting fingers of some of the 10,000 women who, working in factories in pairs, hand-roll an average 5,000 kretek a day. Today nearly 25 per cent of Indonesia's annual output of clove cigarettes is produced in Kudus, a corruption of al-Quds, the Arabic name for Jerusalem, in central Java.

Indonesians today smoke 36,000 tons of cloves a year – far more than they can grow. It is ironic that what was once the world's sole supplier of cloves today cannot even grow enough to meet domestic demand. It now imports cloves from Zanzibar, to where seedlings were smuggled from Ternate in the 1770s, to help fill the gap.

Another irony is that although Indonesia is today the world's largest Muslim nation, its most universal symbol – Borobudur – is the world's biggest Buddhist monument. A terraced pyramid of hewn volcanic rock topped by seventy-two bell-shaped *stupa*, Borobudur was completed in 850, six years before Buddhism was overthrown by Hinduism on Java, and six centuries before it was replaced by Islam. Our 'pilgrimage' to Borobudur was, however, for a secular purpose, for apart from being a great religious monument, Borobudur is an important source of historical information. On its walls are 2,712 pictorial reliefs detailing – besides Buddhist doctrine – life and culture on eighth and ninth century Java. These 8,235 square metres (88,640 square feet) of stone carvings include twelve reliefs depicting early South-East Asian maritime trade. One stone panel sharply delineates in bas relief a ship and its busy crew, while another shows a Spice Route sailor being rescued from the jaws of a fearsome fish.

In contrast with the stone imagery of Borobudur, nearby Yogyakarta, the only princely state that survived the national revolution of 1945–9, is today a living museum. Kraton, the palace that is Yogyakarta's core, is a city within a city, where thousands of people live and work – servants, guards, musicians, jesters, the sultan's retinue and the royal family itself. Insulated within its walls, Yogyakarta is able to maintain the cultural traditions that have faded elsewhere.

Here, for example, we watched an exotic performance of the classical Ramayana Ballet, based on a 2,000-year-old Hindu epic, in which an Indian prince – aided by the king of the birds and an army of apes – defeats the wicked ruler of Lanka and rescues his captive consort. We also listened to the haunting music of a native Gamelan orchestra composed of bronze and bamboo xylophones, gongs and drums.

BUGIS SCHOONERS LINING THE QUAY OF JAKARTA'S SMALL SHIPS HARBOUR RECALL THE ATMOSPHERE OF THE OLD ASIAN TRADING WORLD.

After a brief break on Bali, and a stop-over on Sulawesi – today the world's biggest supplier of nutmegs – we set off for our final destination: the original 'Spice Islands' of Ternate, Tidore, Banda and Ambon. Although spices are now grown in many tropical regions, these islands were once the world's only source of nutmeg, cloves and mace.

To find these obscure islands – situated at the eastern extremity of the Indonesian archipelago, on the western rim of the Pacific Ocean, between the Philippines in the north and Australia in the south – Colombus crossed the Atlantic and Magellan circumnavigated the world. Once they had been 'discovered', the great kingdoms of Europe fought bitterly for control of these tiny islands, and committed some of the worst excesses of colonialism in order to monopolize their precious harvest.

Overflying Banda – a jewel-like cluster of nine lush volcanic islands set in splendid isolation in a crystal-clear tropical sea – it is hard to relate it to the violence, chicanery and tragedy that occurred here. Once we landed, however, the reality became clear: brooding ruins of earthquake-shattered forts recall the ruthless force by which the Dutch imposed their monopoly of the islands' nutmegs, while dilapidated colonial mansions testify to fortunes made from spice – but long since spent.

Even majestic Fire Mountain, which rises in a seemingly perfect cone over Gunung Api island, is not all it looks. Struggling up the volcano's steep slopes to its still-smoking summit, we saw the far side had been obliterated (by a violent eruption in 1988 which killed three people), leaving us standing on the edge of a frightening precipice.

THE WORLD'S LARGEST BUDDHIST MONUMENT AT BOROBUDUR, INDONESIA, ON WHOSE WALLS CARVED STONE PANELS PORTRAY MARITIME TRADE ON JAVA 1,000 YEARS AGO.

Although Banda was once the world's sole supplier of nutmeg, it is now out-produced by other islands to which seedlings were transplanted by the British to break the seventeenth and eighteenth-century Dutch monopoly of the spice trade. Banda now produces only 25 per cent of Indonesia's 75 per cent share of the world nutmeg market, the other 25 per cent coming from the Caribbean island of Grenada.

In fact the nutmeg seems to have brought Banda little but greed, graft and grief, for in order to establish a plantation system, the Dutch East Indies Company (the VOC) either slaughtered or enslaved the islanders, and razed their villages to force them to flee, while the monopoly the VOC imposed was ultimately self-defeating. It encouraged plantation managers – licensed Dutch farmers who received only a one-hundred-and-twenty-secondth of the going rate of nutmeg in Europe – to cheat whenever possible. Rampant smuggling and the high cost of maintaining garrisons to enforce the monopoly cut deeply into VOC's profits too, so that finally, in the closing years of the eighteenth century, the company went bankrupt causing economic chaos, neglect and decline.

Even today the concepts of trade monopoly and cheap labour still permeate the islands' economy, and the plantation system – with all its faults – persists. Eighty per cent of Banda's nutmeg groves are owned by the central government, and although workers receive half of their crop in payment, they must sell their share back to the state at less than the fair market price.

But although production has dropped dramatically – many trees were cut down during the Japanese occupation of the islands in the Second World War – nutmeg and mace remain the mainstay of Banda's fragile economy. Patches of crimson mace and golden brown nutmeg drying in the sun are a common – and colourful – sight.

Looked after properly, the sensitive nutmeg tree – usually planted in groves protected by tall kanari trees – will bear fruit for sixty years or longer. The nutmeg fruit is picked with a long pole tipped with a basket, and the network of mace surrounding the shell removed, flattened and laid out to dry in the sun. The shell too is gradually sun-dried, and turned twice daily over a period of eight weeks until the seed – or nutmeg – rattles

inside when shaken. The shell is then broken with a wooden truncheon and the nutmeg picked out.

Nutmeg and mace were introduced to international emporia by Javanese traders, and first reached Europe, via India and the Near East, in about A.D. 500. By the ninth century, the Arabs were making regular year-and-a-half long trading voyages from the Arabian Gulf to the south China coast and back again, with all the exotica of the Orient, including spices. By the fourteenth century, they had sailed as far as the Spice Islands themselves to trade rice and cloth for nutmeg, mace and cloves.

The first Europeans to reach the Spice Islands were the Portuguese. They visited Banda in 1512, but did not stay there, basing themselves instead on the clove-growing island of Ternate further north. With a final sweep over Banda's rusting tin rooftops we too headed north, stopping over briefly on the island of Seram – on a second attempt; the first landing being abruptly aborted when a herd of cows crossed the runway right in front of our tiny Otter aircraft.

An even bigger jolt, however, awaited photographer Nik Wheeler on Ternate. Searching the foothills of the still-active Gamalama volcano, which dominates the island, for the world's 'oldest' clove tree, he fell headlong into a ravine, smashing a camera, scarring his shoulder and scraping his face. We never did find the reputedly 400-year-old clove tree, but I did discover through further research that the history of cloves goes back much further – in fact as far back as the early Han dynasty of China (206 B.C.–A.D. 200), whose annals record that cloves were customarily held in the mouth to perfume the breath during audiences with the emperor.

Scholars believe cloves reached China via the Philippines, and it was via the Philippines too that the second group of Europeans – the Spanish – reached the Spice Islands hot on the heels of the Portuguese. By the fifteenth century, according to an account written in England, a kilogram of mace was worth as much as a cow, and a ship laden with spices from the East could make enough profit to pay ten times the cost of the voyage, including the value of the ship itself.

CHILDREN PLAY AMONG THE RUINS OF FORT TOKOLO ON TERNATE, WHERE PORTUGUESE, SPANISH AND DUTCH FOUGHT EACH OTHER FOR CONTROL OF THE ISLAND'S LUCRATIVE CLOVE TRADE.

While the Portuguese reached the Spice Islands by sailing around Africa and across the Indian Ocean, Magellan – under the flag of Spain – came from the opposite direction: across the Atlantic, then the Pacific, to the Philippines. Although it cost Magellan his life and four of his five ships to find the Spice Islands, one vessel – the *Victoria* – loaded with cloves from Tidore did return westwards to Spain to become the first ship ever to circumnavigate the globe.

For us, however, it was but a brief boat-ride from Ternate to Tidore, less than 1 kilometre (0.6 miles) away. Across this narrow strait the Portuguese, entrenched in Ternate, and the Spanish, on Tidore, jostled each other and the islands' rival sultans for almost a century for control of the spice trade. Finally, in 1599, the arrival of the Dutch forced both Iberian powers to leave, and reduced the once-wealthy sultanates to ruin. First the Dutch allied themselves with Ternate against Tidore to control the clove trade, then they wiped out nearly all the trees on Ternate to monopolize it, confining clove production to Ambon, where the monopoly could be enforced more effectively.

The forts that once bristled on Ternate – according to one guidebook, more fortification per square metre than anywhere else in Indonesia – are now mostly overgrown ruins, their walls breached by time, and in the case of the seaside Fort Kalimaka, also by the tide. Today, despite its tempestuous history and the repeated rumblings of Gamalama – it last erupted in 1990 – Ternate has a friendly, bustling air, having regained its status as a major clove producer.

Propagated from seeds planted in shaded areas, the clove tree attains a height of up to 15 metres (50 feet), and begins flowering in its fifth year. One tree can yield up to 34 kilograms (75 pounds) of unopened buds, which are hand-picked twice a year, using bamboo ladders and scaffolding, lowered to the ground in baskets and sun dried.

FRUIT OF THE NUTMEG TREE, WHOSE AROMATIC SEED IS GROUND INTO SPICE.

Although it was once the world's main source of supply, Ternate today provides cloves only for locally-produced and consumed clove cigarettes, the world's main suppliers now being the African islands of Zanzibar and Pemba, to where seedlings were smuggled from Ternate to break the Dutch monopoly. Surprisingly too, the spices – nutmeg, mace and cloves – that made the Spice Islands famous are seldom used in local cuisine. In fact, our most memorable meal in South-East Asia contained no spices at all: freshly boiled Ternatian coconut crab, whose giant claws – used to crack open the coconuts it feeds on – are big enough to fill one person's stomach.

With our palate, as well as ourselves, somewhat jaded after three months retracing the Spice Route, we arrived at last at our final destination, Ambon. It was somewhat of an anticlimax. Now, as in the heyday of the spice trade, it is the administrative centre of the Moluccas – as the eastern islands of Indonesia are known – but today, Ambon holds few physical charms.

The so-called 'jewel' of the Dutch spice empire for almost 200 years after the VOC concentrated clove production there, Ambon became a forgotten backwater once the company went bankrupt in 1799. What was left of its old colonial buildings, parks, squares and tree-lined waterfront after 150 years of genteel decline was destroyed by allied bombers in raids against the Japanese occupiers in August 1949. Today, low rectangular buildings covered with coloured metal cladding sully Ambon's city centre, and drab modern buildings disfigure the surrounding hills.

So with hardly a backward glance at the last of the legendary Spice Islands we had travelled so far to see, we began our journey home via Hong Kong. Our adventures – or rather Wheeler's misadventures – were not over, however. While Hong Kong greeted the Chinese New Year with a dazzling fireworks display, Nik suddenly succumbed to a raging tropical fever, and it was all we could do to get him home to Los Angeles next day and into hospital.

Wheeler did eventually recover, but his illness served as a grim reminder of one of the many hazards endured by the merchant-adventurers of old. Although our journey retracing the Spice Route no way matched theirs, we too had sought adventure – and found more than we bargained for.

SPICE
GLOSSARY

The English word 'spices' derives from the Latin species, indicative of the many varieties available. The dominant species of the spice trade included cinnamon, cloves, ginger, nutmeg and pepper, which are dried parts of various plants of tropical and subtropical regions.

The most notable uses of spices in very early times were in medicine, magical rites and religious rituals. Pliny the Elder, in his first century A.D. Natural History, extols at length the efficacy and healing powers of spices and herbs in the treatment of just about every aliment known in his day.

Cloves, pepper and ginger came into use in medieval Europe in the twelfth century, and from that time onwards no banquet was completed without spiced dishes. They were, however, beyond the purse of most people. An account written in England in 1418 reveals that half a kilogram of ginger cost as much as a sheep, and a kilogram of mace as much as a cow.

Modern uses of spices are legion; there are few culinary recipes that do not include them. In medicine spices have not entirely lost their reputation; in India and other Asiatic countries their curative virtues still enjoy respect.

CINNAMON

is the dried inner bark of the laurel Cinnamomum zeylanicum, native to the island of Sri Lanka, the Malabar coast of India, Burma and China, where it was first noted in 2700 B.C. The best grade of cinnamon is that stripped off in May and June when the bark is full of sap. Cassia, which is held to be somewhat inferior to cinnamon, is the basis of most modern ground cinnamon, but only true connoisseurs can distinguish it from the superior type.

CLOVES

are the unopened flower buds of the tropical evergreen
Syzygium aromatica, native to the Moluccas, or Spice Islands, of Indonesia.
These nail-shaped buds – the English 'clove' comes from the French clou,
or 'nail' – are hand-picked in the late summer and again in winter, sun-dried and used
whole or ground. In the seventeenth century the Dutch tried to gain control of the clove
trade by eliminating the trees from all but two islands, Ternate and Ambo, but a Frenchman
with the 'spicy' name of Pierre Poivre – Peter Pepper – broke the Dutch monopoly by smuggling
clove seedlings to islands in the Indian Ocean and the New World, where production today is
concentrated in Malagasy and Zanzibar.

GINGER

is the pungent underground stem, or rhizome, of the herbaceous perennial plant Zingiber
officinali, native to India and South-East Asia. Harvesting is done simply by lifting the
rhizomes from the soil, cleansing them and drying them in the sun. South-East Asian
mariners took potted ginger on early sea voyages to ward off scurvy. In Japan, slices of
ginger are eaten between courses to clear the palate. The spice was introduced into Europe in
Roman times, and became very popular as a food flavouring. It was also used medicinally.
Elizabeth I of England is said to have invented that all-time favourite the gingerbread man
when she ordered small ginger-flavoured cakes made in the shapes of her courtiers.

NUTMEG

is the seed of the dioecious evergreen Myristica fragrans, native to the Moluccas,
or Spice Islands, of Indonesia. The fleshy yellow peach-like fruit of this tree
splits open when ripe, revealing the nutmeg encased in a dark brown shell,
encircled by a network of crimson mace. The hard aromatic nut
or seed of the tree is ground into the familiar spice.
Less known, but even more valuable, is mace,
a spice prepared from the bright red
waxy lace that covers this nut.
Nutmeg trees are sensitive,
and are cultivated in groves
protected by tall kanari trees.
Even today the specific conditions
required for the nutmeg tree to survive – moist air
and light volcanic soil – exist only in Indonesia and
Grenada.

PEPPER

is the small berry-like fruit, or peppercorn, of the
perennial climbing vine Piper nigrum, native to southern
India, particularly the Malabar coast. Probably the most widely used
spice in the world today, pepper is also cultivated for export in
Indonesia, Cambodia, Sri Lanka, Malagasy, Malaysia, Thailand and
Brazil. The whole peppercorns when ground yield black pepper; white
pepper is obtained from peppercorns with the outer part removed. In
medieval England peppercorns were used to pay rents, taxes, tolls and
wedding dowries; and were considered so precious they were counted
out one by one.

THE INCENSE TRAIL

ANCIENT COLUMNS
LINE A SECTION OF
ROMAN ROAD AT
PETRA, NORTHERN
TERMINUS OF THE
INCENSE TRAIL.

The oldest international caravan route in the world was the Incense Trail. It linked the aromatic growing regions of Arabia with the incense-craving empires of the ancient world, including Egypt, Babylon and Rome. The legendary Queen of Sheba journeyed along this route to meet King Solomon, and the Three Wise Men bore along it gifts of gold, frankincense and myrrh.

Though frankincense and myrrh were gifts given in the Christmas story to the Jesus child, few people realise that incense then was just as valuable as gold. For as Arab historian al-Tabri said, in explaining the offerings of the Three Wise Men, 'the smoke of incense reaches heaven as does no other smoke'.

The resin of the frankincense tree, *Boswellia sacra*, is one of a number of aromatic substances that, like myrrh and aloes wood, give off a pungent, pleasurable smell when burned. This seemingly minor characteristic was esteemed so highly in ancient cultures that almost all the peoples of the Mediterranean and the Middle East considered it vital to their religious rituals. They believed the fragrant white smoke from incense soothed angry gods.

The Temple of Baal in Babylon, for example, burned two and a half tons of frankincense a year, according to ancient records, while wall carvings at Karnak show the Egyptian Pharaoh Rameses II (circa 1224 B.C.) offering incense before the Sacred Barge. He carries a triple incense burner in his left hand, and with his right he throws grains of incense onto it, their trajectory indicated by a curve of dots. Hawk-headed priests carry the barge in ranks of five, pacing backward and forward and announcing the will of Amon.

Besides religious rituals, incense was also used in funerary rites; Pliny says the emperor Nero burned an entire year's production of incense from Arabia at the funeral of his wife Poppaea. Frankincense was used for embalming corpses – pellets of frankincense were found in King Tutankhamun's tomb – and Celsus, the first-century Roman medical writer, says the ancient Greeks used frankincense to treat haemorrhoids.

Produced in Southern Arabia and the Horn of Africa, and exported across northern Arabia to Petra in Jordan, incense was as important to the economy of the Middle East as oil is today. From Petra it was transported west across Sinai to Egypt, north via Gaza to Rome, and east via Palmyra to Mesopotamia, where an incense burner found in the ruins of an al'Ubaid-period temple at Tepe Gawra, near Mosul in northern Iraq, dates incense's earliest use there to around 3500 B.C.

By the time Roman power was established in the Levant, the final legs of the route were controlled by Syrian traders operating under Rome's aegis. Palmyra alone preserved its independence from Rome, and played a pivotal role in international trade: a desert port for caravans entering and leaving Mesopotamia, and a junction of the Silk Road and the Incense Trail. It was here we began our journey along the latter.

Palmyra – city of palms – was known in the Bible as Tadmor, and that is its name in Arabic today. Inscriptions found there indicate that the population was mixed and that the inhabitants spoke Aramaic, Greek and Latin. A large colony of merchants from northern Arabia occupied a quarter of the city.

Palmyreans were above all caravan operators, acting as intermediaries for goods coming from Arabia and Africa along the Incense Trail, or from Parthia and Central Asia by way of the Silk Road. From Palmyra, and still by Palmyrean caravans, the goods then proceeded to Antioch and Seleucia in Syria, and down the Euphrates to the Persian Gulf. As the Parthians long refused to trade directly with Rome, all commerce had to pass by way of Palmyra, and this little kingdom endured as an intermediary and buffer-state for more than two centuries.

'Palmyra,' wrote Pliny, 'a town famous for its situation, the richness of its soil and its agreeable waters, is surrounded by a vast belt of sand. Virtually cut off by nature from the rest of the world, she enjoys independence though lying between the two powerful empires of Rome and Parthia. When there is discord the first thoughts of both of these are for her.'

The Romans, who from the first century B.C. had been moving eastward in a series of campaigns that would eventually bring much of the Middle East under their control, absorbed Petra into their orbit in the first century A.D. But Palmyra proved difficult to digest. In the third century Odenathus, a prince of Palmyra, built a strong autonomous state embracing all of Syria, northwestern Mesopotamia and western Armenia. Odenathus' wife Zenobia, apparently of Arab stock to judge by her name (Zaynab), took the reins after his death and aggressively expanded Palmyrene power into Asia Minor, Mesopotamia and Egypt. Declaring her son emperor, she even had coins struck bearing his portrait and her own. This was too much for Rome – it meant the loss of the entire Eastern Empire – and in 272 Aurelian was sent to attack Palmyra. He destroyed Palmyrene power, captured Zenobia, and brought her to Rome decked in golden chains. She was then pensioned off and ended her days confined in a Roman villa.

Crossing the Syrian desert that surrounds the spectacular ruins of Palmyra, I drove across northern Jordan to Amman to join the Kings' Highway. One of the most historic and scenic roads in the Middle East, this route links Amman, the original Philadelphia of 2,000 years ago, with Aqaba on the Red Sea. Along this route, in use since 3000 B.C., are Petra, rock-carved capital of the Nabatean Arabs; commanding Crusader castles at Karak and Shobak; and a litany of Biblical sites, including Machaerus – present-day Mukawir – where Salome danced and John the Baptist lost his head. Parts of the road paved by the Romans are still visible in places today.

The route is at its most spectacular when it plunges through the gorges of Wadi al-Hasa and Wadi Mujib; the latter, about 3,000 metres (almost 2 miles) wide and 1,440 metres (4,600 feet) deep, is comparable to the United States' Grand Canyon.

Leaving Amman, now the modern capital of Jordan, at dawn we drove through Madaba – believed inhabited for over 4,500 years – and as the sun rose, climbed slowly out of Wadi Mujib. In mid-morning we paused for Turkish coffee beneath the glowering walls of Karak Castle, the most important Crusader stronghold in Jordan. By mid-afternoon we were clambering over the battered battlements of Shobak fortress, built on a mountain of rock by the Crusader Baldwin I, King of Jerusalem, in about 1115 and captured in 1189 by Salah al-Din, or Saladin. As the sun set at Petra we walked through the Shiqq, the winding fissure between overhanging cliffs which suddenly opens out into a hidden valley lined with temples, 'treasure houses' and tombs carved into the salmon-pink rock by the Nabateans some 2,300 years ago. We had traversed 5,000 years of history in the course of a single day.

For thousands of years Aqaba complemented the commercial activities of Petra – the nearby capital of the Nabateans – and the trade routes of Wadi Rum. Today it plays a similar role, as Jordan's only port, and a year-round resort complementing visits to Petra's archeological treasures with a relaxing interlude by the sea.

ONE OF THE MANY TREASURE HOUSES, TEMPLES AND TOMBS CARVED INTO CLIFFS OF THE HIDDEN VALLEY OF PETRA.

AN ELDERLY ARAB RESTS BESIDE THE KINGS' HIGHWAY, WHICH LINKS THE JORDANIAN CAPITAL OF AMMAN WITH AQABA, THE COUNTRY'S LARGEST PORT.

According to conventional wisdom the Nabateans were exclusively desert people, who ruled the caravan routes of present-day Jordan and northwest Saudi Arabia, but careful scrutiny of ancient historical accounts shows the Nabateans had a far greater maritime capability than is generally realized. This early Arab people possessed not only a merchant shipping capability but a naval fleet as well.

According to the Greek historian Plutarch, the Nabatean navy destroyed by fire a fleet of Egyptian galleys, thus frustrating an attempt by Cleopatra to establish a naval presence on the Red Sea. Through military or diplomatic agreements the Nabateans were welcome in the ports of Hatra, on the Euphrates, Gerrha, on the west coast of the Arabian Gulf, and Ascalon, on the Mediterranean coast of Palestine. Nabatean seafarers were also frequent visitors in Alexandria, Miletus in Asia Minor, and the Roman port of Puteoli near Naples. These maritime activities could explain a phenomenon that has puzzled archaeologists for some time: the frequent use in the sculptures and inscriptions of Petra of dolphin imagery, regarded as a good luck symbol by sailors even in ancient times.

Driving south from Petra along Wadi Rum – today a vast, silent landscape of ancient river beds and stretches of sandy desert flanked by towering sandstone cliffs – it was hard to imagine that this was once the main thoroughfare along which flowed north much of the rich incense trade, for all that remains is Thamudic graffiti scratched by centuries of camel drivers on large boulders by the little-travelled trail. The Thamud tribe had its centre near Madain Saleh, in present-day Saudi Arabia, and their script belongs to the southern Semitic group of alphabets, the only surviving example of which is Ethiopian.

Modern highways linking Jordan and Saudi Arabia bypass Wadi Rum, and after having had twice to dig our Land Rover out of its sands we did likewise, taking the coastal road along the Gulf of Aqaba to Tabuk. It was here, two years before he died, that the Prophet Muhammad concluded treaties with the tribes of northwestern Arabia – an event that not only established Islam throughout the peninsula, but also opened the way for Islam's thrust west into Byzantine-controlled Palestine and beyond.

Muslim and Byzantine armies first crossed swords in 632 at Mu'tah, in Jordan, when Zayd ibn Harithah, one of Muhammad's closest companions, led 3,000 men out of Arabia to avenge the death of a Muslim envoy executed by the Ghassanids, Christian Arabs who were clients of the Byzantines. The battle ended disastrously for the Muslims: Zayd and two other leaders who subsequently took command were all slain, leaving the newly converted Khalid ibn al-Walid to lead the shattered remnants of the Muslim army back home. The Muslim setback at Mu'tah was only temporary, and in the years immediately following the death of Muhammad, Egypt, Syria, Mesopotamia, most of Asia Minor and Persia were conquered.

Our route from Tabuk to Madinah followed that of the now-abandoned Hizaj railroad, built at the beginning of this century by the Ottoman Turks to link the holy cities of Western Arabia. It in turn followed the earlier route of camel caravans, which once carried pilgrims to Makkah, the holiest city of Islam.

Sandstone railroad stations built by the Turks, when Arabia was part of the Ottoman Empire, still dot the harsh desert landscape of the Hijaz. Some of them have been carefully restored, with shiny black steam locomotives resting silently in repair sheds. There is even evidence of the original pilgrim caravan route: at Madain Saleh stands a restored medieval way-station built to accommodate pilgrims, caravan crews and their animals travelling to Makkah.

Although we searched for the 'lost city' of Leuce Come, a Nabatean port that ancient writers said served as a key transhipment point for incense and other goods en route to the

WADI RUM, LINKING JORDAN AND SAUDI ARABIA, WAS ONCE THE MAIN THOROUGHFARE ALONG WHICH PASSED MUCH OF ARABIA'S RICH INCENSE TRADE.

Mediterranean from Southern Arabia, we could find no evidence of it. Its existence is first testified to by Strabo, and later by the author of *The Periplus of the Erythrean Sea*, but despite various theories as to where Leuce Come might have been, contemporary explorers and archaeologists have been unable to locate it.

According to Strabo, Roman legionnaries who invaded Arabia in 24 B.C. in a failed attempt to break Arab control of the incense trade landed at Leuce Come – 'a large emporium in the land of the Nabateans' – fourteen days after setting sail from Cleopatris (Suez) in Egypt. The *Periplus* places Leuce Come 'two or three days (sailing) from Mussel Harbour (al-Qusayr) eastwards across the adjacent gulf (the Red Sea)'. Despite these geographic indicators some scholars say Leuce Come was probably located on the site of present-day Yanbu, which seemed to us to be obviously too far south, while others identify it with ruins at Aynunah, at the head of the Red Sea – too far north.

The American scholar Wilfred Schoff – whose translation of *Periplus* is quoted above – placed Leuce Come at al-Haura, midway between Yanbu and al-Wajh, but this location too is not consistent with Strabo, who says the Roman legions passed through Hijr – 200 kilometres (125 miles) northeast of al-Haura – on the way back to their sea transport at Leuce Come. If al-Haura had indeed been Leuce Come this would have been a curiously circuitous route to reach it.

A more natural port for Hijr would have been at or near modern al-Wajh, which is the nearest point on the coast to Hijr. Al-Wajh also fits *Periplus's* placement of Leuce Come – eastwards across the Red Sea from al-Qusayr. But even at al-Wajh – a picturesque little port with gaily painted fishing boats at anchor in the shadow of a small mosque – we found no trace of Leuce Come. So heading inland we retraced the probable tracks of the Roman legionnaries; following sandy trails and rutted tracks along winding wadi beds through the Hijaz mountain range to Hijr, known today as Madain Saleh.

Classical Arab geographers such as Al-Idrisi, Al-Mogaddissi and Al-Istakhri identify Hijr as the Thamudic homeland, but it is to the later Nabatean period of the first century B.C. that the magnificent monumental architecture visible today at Madain Saleh belongs. Here the Nabateans carved monumental tombs out of sandstone cliffs, often imitating Egyptian, Greek or Roman architectural styles. Today only the imposing temple-like facades of the now-empty tombs adorn the cliff faces of Madain Saleh.

The Nabateans controlled the northern portion of the rich trade routes, running up the western coast of Arabia as far as Jordan, and Madain Saleh is believed to have stood on the frontier they shared with the southern Arabians, who controlled the trade routes as far south as Yemen. It was these latter routes we now followed: first through black volcanic hills to Madinah, once a busy crossroads for the camel caravans that were the lifeblood of Arabia, and today the second holiest city of Islam.

It was here, in the mid-620s, that the Prophet Muhammad established an Islamic city-state that was to become the springboard for the worldwide spread of Islam – now the religion of over a billion people. Madinah was an important stage on the Incense Trail, and Muhammad himself is said to have engaged in the caravan trade with Syria. When Muhammad died in Madinah in 632, Islam was still restricted to Arabia, but he had already inspired his followers with a fiery zeal that enabled them to conquer the Persian and Byzantine empires and many lands beyond.

After Saudi photographer Abdullah Dobais had prayed at the Prophet's Mosque, where Muhammad is buried, we set off across a sandy coastal plain to Jiddah. Formerly a quiet seaport under Ottoman suzerainty, with a population of 30,000 living within an area of a few square kilometres, Jiddah is now a mega-metropolis and ultra-modern seaport. Today it has a population of over 1.5 million spread over some 400 square kilometres (154 square miles).

THE PROPHET'S MOSQUE AT MADINAH, SAUDI ARABIA, A MAJOR CARAVAN CROSSROADS AND SPRINGBOARD FOR THE WORLDWIDE SPREAD OF ISLAM.

© S. M. AMIN

An eight-lane highway runs inland from Jiddah across the coastal plain towards Makkah (Mecca), the holiest city of Islam and forbidden for non-Muslims to enter. About 24 kilometres (15 miles) before Makkah a sign reads 'Muslims only'. The road splits and non-Muslims are guided around the holy city towards the mountains. The non-Muslim road becomes a single carriageway, cutting a 30-mile detour south of Makkah across a plain strewn with boulders scoured clean by sand storms. Wild camels graze on the roadside. The road starts to climb the steep rocky outcrops and rejoins the main highway east of Mecca.

This is Route 15, which rides the ridge of the Asir Mountains, snaking south through a series of switchbacks. The road clings precariously to the mountainside and at one point seems to leave it completely, supported by concrete struts. Once it reaches Al-Hada, a tourist resort at about 6,500 feet, the road runs southeast towards Abha, a seven-hour drive away through a national park. Baboons watched us as we drove by en route to southern Arabia.

Brought from Dhofar, in present-day Oman, and from the Horn of Africa to Yemen by sea, and then transported overland by camel caravan, incense brought prosperity to southern Arabia. All this rich trade paid its dues to the Arabian kingdoms whose territory it crossed in the form of taxes, duties and transit tolls, as well as commissions to the Arab merchants who transported it. Mighty kingdoms – Sheba in Yemen and Nabatea in Saudi Arabia – flourished from their trade.

Myrrh came mainly from Somalia and Ethiopia. Frankincense was the basis of the economy of Oman's Dhofar province for over 2,000 years. It peaked in the first and second centuries A.D., when King Il'ad Yalut of the Hadhramaut took over the incense-producing areas, built the port of Sumhuram, near Salalah, and so secured a monopoly of the frankincense trade. With the decline of the Roman Empire, the demand for incense slackened somewhat; though Christians also used incense at mass and other ceremonies, the quantities were comparatively small. Another reason was the problem of finding enough people willing to tackle the difficult work involved in collecting the frankincense resin.

Frankincense collection – which begins in winter, peaks in spring and ends with the summer monsoons – starts with shaving strips of bark from the *Boswellia sacra* trunk. The collectors use an instrument like a putty knife called a *mingaf*. From these wounds the frankincense resin, or *luban*, oozes out and hardens into crystals, which are scraped off the tree and collected in two-handled baskets of woven palm leaves. Even better, frankincense – light and clean in colour – can be obtained by simply waiting and collecting it from the ground after it has fallen from the tree and dried naturally.

As recently as 1946 some 2,800 tons of various kinds of aromatic gums and resins – including frankincense – were being handled by the merchants of Aden, but in that year an artificial substitute was developed in Rome, delivering the *coup de grâce* for Oman's frankincense trade. The substitute involved cheap chemicals, which were melded into a shiny, rock-like conglomerate and distributed in brown chunks that had to be broken apart by a hammer. It was unappealing. It lacked the mystic feel of the East. And its smoke was by no means as white. But it smelled exactly like frankincense – and cost much less. 'Since then,' laments a Salalah merchant, 'trade in incense has become only a fraction of what it used to be.'

What little is left of the frankincense trade today is mainly in the hands of the Bait Kathir, and to a lesser degree al-Mahra, tribes in whose territories – the desert plateau above Salalah – frankincense trees still grow, but even they no longer work at it with any diligence. Recently, for example, during what should have been the height of the season, I drove to the plateau and found no one at all collecting frankincense. So I took a penknife and scraped the bark of a gnarled old frankincense tree, then rested in the shade of its low twisted branches while its resin oozed out and hardened. An hour later, I walked off with a pocketful of crystals. Once worth their weight in gold, they had not cost me a penny.

INDEX

A

ABBASID — 80, 93
ACEH — 3, 8, 107
ACHAEMENIDS — 16
ADAM'S PEAK — 99, 102
AFGHANISTAN — 11, 13, 15, 26–27, 31, 37–38, 40–41, 44–46, 67
AGA KHAN DEVELOPMENT NETWORK — 40
AGA KHAN TRUST FOR CULTURE — 47
AEGEAN SEA — 16–17
AI KHANOUM — 40, 41
AKKADIANS — 75
AKSUM — 84
ALEXANDER THE GREAT — 16, 25–26, 41, 45, 47, 55, 79, 81
ALEXANDRIA — 79–80, 83, 88, 102, 120
ALFONSO DE ALBUQUERQUE — 94
AL-MAQADISI — 88
AL-QUSAYR — 80, 83, 121
ALTAI MOUNTAINS — 52, 53–55, 61
ALTAI TURKS — 51, 55
AL-WAJH — 121
AMBON — 79, 111, 113
AMMAN — 118
ANATOLIA — 13, 15–21
ANKARA — 17, 21, 31
ANTIOCH — 88, 118
AQABA — 118
ARABIAN GULF — 16, 20, 80, 87–88, 120
ARABIAN PENINSULA — 81, 83, 84, 95
ARABIAN SEA — 79, 87–95, 99, 103
ARABS — 16, 23, 26–27, 75, 81, 83, 87, 103
ARARAT, Mount — 21
ARMENIA — 22, 118
ASSYRIANS — 13, 17, 19, 53, 76
ATTILA — 51, 53, 70
AUGUSTUS, Emperor — 83, 95
AUREL STEIN — 71
AZERBAIJAN — 21, 23, 33, 34

B

BABUR — 44, 45
BABYLON — 19, 45, 117
BACTRIAN CAMEL — 11, 48
BADAKHSHAN — 40
BAGH-E-BABUR — 44
BAGHDAD — 31, 87, 88, 93, 102
BAKU — 23
BALTIT FORT — 47
BAMIYAN VALLEY — 40, 41
BANDA — 3, 79, 105, 111–12
BARBARICUM — 84, 89
BARYGAZA — 84, 89, 93
BAY OF BENGAL — 45, 95, 103
BEGRAM PLAIN — 41
BEGRAM TREASURE — 44, 46
BEIJING (Khanbalik) — 61
BEZEKLIK — 68
BIBI KHANUM MOSQUE — 31
BLACK SEA — 15, 20–23, 26, 31, 52–53, 55, 60

BOMBAY — 93–94
BOROBODUR — 76, 110, 111
BOSPHORUS — 15, 16, 23
BRITISH — 45, 47–48, 68, 94, 95, 97, 99, 103, 105, 107, 111
BRITISH EAST INDIA COMPANY — 94, 103, 110
BUDDHA — 40, 45, 46, 61, 63, 73
BUDDHISM — 9, 12, 23, 41, 45, 46, 55, 56, 60, 61, 63, 67, 68, 72, 73, 75, 105, 110, 111
BUKHARA — 8, 11, 24, 25, 26, 27, 30, 33, 93
BYZANTINE EMPIRE — 11, 13, 16, 17, 21, 22, 23, 26, 71, 84, 120, 121
BYZANTIUM — 11, 15, 16, 30

C

CALICUT — 95, 97
CAMBAY — 89, 93
CANA — 84
CAPPADOCIA — 19–20
CARAVANSERAIS — 12, 15, 19, 21, 45
CARRHAE, Battle of — 20
CASPIAN SEA — 11, 23, 31, 63
CAUCASUS — 13, 22–23, 55
CELESTIAL HORSES — 34, 37
CENTRAL ASIA — 9, 12, 13, 15, 25, 26, 27, 30–31, 33–34, 37–38, 40, 41, 44, 45, 46, 48, 51, 56, 57, 60, 61, 63, 66, 67, 70, 71, 87, 92, 93, 118
CHINA — 5, 9, 11–13, 16, 23, 25–27, 31, 33–34, 37–38, 41, 44, 46–48, 51–53, 55–57, 60–61, 63, 65–68, 70–73, 75, 84, 87–89, 93, 95, 103, 105, 112, 115
CHINESE — 9, 11–13, 23, 26–27, 33, 37–38, 40–41, 44, 46–48, 51–53, 55–56, 60–61, 63, 65–68, 70–71, 73, 75, 95, 97, 102–03, 105, 113
CHRISTIANITY — 12, 16, 23, 67–68, 75, 95
CINNAMON — 76, 79–81, 83, 102, 114
CLEOPATRA — 79, 120
CLOVES — 75, 79, 105, 107, 110–15
COCHIN — 75, 95, 97
COLOMBUS — 111
CONSTANTINE — 15
CONSTANTINOPLE — 15, 30, 84
COPTUS — 80, 83
CRANGANORE (Muziris) — 84, 95
CRESUS — 16
CRUSADERS — 118

D

DAMASCUS — 20, 31
DARIUS — 16
DEBAL — 89
DEER STONES — 55
DHOFAR — 123
DHOW — 87–89, 95, 97, 105
DIONYSIUS CASSIUS — 20
DOGUBEYAZIT — 21
DUNHUANG — 73
DUTCH — 95, 97, 99, 102–03, 105, 107, 110–13, 115
DUTCH EAST INDIA COMPANY — 103, 110

E

EGYPT 9, 12, 17, 20, 40, 44, 76, 79–81, 83–84, 87, 89, 107, 117–18, 120–21
ERDENE ZUU MONASTERY 60, 61
ERZURUM 21–22
EUDAEMON (Aden) 81, 84, 123
EUPHRATES 19, 20
EURASIA 19–20, 88, 118, 120
EURASIAN STEPPE 13, 34, 38, 51, 53, 61, 125

F

FERGHANA VALLEY 11, 34, 37
FLECKER, JAMES ELROY 25
FLORUS 20
FRANCIS XAVIER 105
FRANKINCENSE 12, 84, 117, 123
FRIAR WILLIAM OF RUBRUCK 60

G

GALLE 79, 103
GANDHARA 45–46
GANSU CORRIDOR 68, 70
GAOCHANG 66
GENGHIS KHAN 12, 30–31, 44, 51, 61, 63, 93
GEORGIA 21–23, 31
GER (Yurt) 55–57, 61
GERRHAEANS 81
GHAZNAVIDS 30
GHURID CONQUESTS 30
GILGIT 46–47
GINGER 79, 97, 114–15
GOA (Gowapur) 79, 94–95
GOBI DESERT 65, 68, 70
GOLDEN HORDE 33, 37, 56
GOLDEN ROAD 25
GREAT GAME 34, 47–48
GREAT TRUNK ROAD 41, 45–46
GREAT WALL OF CHINA 11, 13, 25, 31, 53, 68, 70
GREEKS 15, 17, 25, 27, 40–41, 45, 47, 55, 57, 76, 79–81, 83, 95, 117–118, 120–21
GUJARAT 89, 93, 94

H

HAN DYNASTY 13, 66, 70–71, 112
HARRAN 20
HATSHEPSUT, Queen 80
HERAT 27, 41
HERODOTUS 17, 79
HIJAZ 120–21
HIMALAYAS 37, 45–46
HINDU KUSH 37, 40–41, 44
HINDUISM 30, 87, 93, 94, 110
HITTITES 17, 19
HOVD 52, 56
HSIUNG-NU 53, 55, 57, 70
HSUAN-TSANG 41
HUNS 7, 37, 51, 53, 55, 57, 70
HUNZA VALLEY 47
HUNZAKUTS 47
HURGOS 38

I

IBN AL-QASIM 89
IBN BATTUTA 89, 93–94
IBN SINA (Avicenna) 25

IL'AD YALUT, King 84, 123
ILI VALLEY 38
IMPERIAL HIGHWAY 13, 40, 65, 70
INCENSE TRAIL 5, 9, 117–18, 121
INDIA 9, 11–13, 23, 25, 27, 30–31, 38, 40–41, 44–65, 55, 67, 75–76, 79–81, 83–84, 87–89, 93–95, 97, 99, 102, 105, 112, 114–115
INDIANS 76, 81, 87
INDIAN OCEAN 3, 75, 84, 87–89, 94–95, 97, 99, 102–03, 105, 113, 115
INDONESIA 75–76, 79, 87, 89, 95, 105, 107, 110–11, 113, 115
INDUS 16, 31, 40–41, 88–89
IRAN 11, 16–17, 21, 26, 27, 34, 41, 63, 84, 88
IRAQ 19, 80, 88, 117
ISHAK PASHA PALACE 21–22
ISLAM 9, 12, 16, 23, 26, 30, 56, 66, 68, 73, 75, 84, 87, 95, 97 105, 110, 120–21, 12
ISSUS, Battle of 16
ISTANBUL 15–16, 21, 84

J

JAISALMER 90–91, 93–94
JAKARTA 107, 110
JAVA 107, 110–11
JERUSALEM 20, 79, 110, 118
JIAOHE 66–67
JIAYUGUAN FORTRESS 70
JIDDAH 83, 121, 123
JORDAN 117–18, 120–21
JULIUS CAESAR 20
JUNKS 8, 89, 97, 105

K

KABUL 40–41, 44–45
KALYAN TOWER 30, 33
KANESH (Kultepe) 17, 19
KAPISA 40, 41, 44
KARA KUM DESERT 26
KARABALGASUN 60
KARAKHANID TURKS 30
KARAKORAM 60–61
KARAKORAM HIGHWAY 15, 46–47
KARAKORUM MOUNTAINS 37–38, 46–47, 65
KARS 21
KASHGAR 15, 46, 48, 65
KAYSERI 17, 19–20
KAZAKHS 30, 37
KAZAKSTAN 11, 13, 23, 33–34, 38, 52, 55
KERALA 87, 95, 97
KHOTAN 65, 71
KHUNJERAB PASS 46–47
KHYBER PASS 30–31, 44–45
KINGS' HIGHWAY 118
KHIVA 33
KHOCHO 66, 68
KOKAND 33
KUBLAI KHAN 61, 75, 97
KUDUS 79, 110
KUL TEGIN 51
KUNLUN MOUNTAINS 65
KURGAN 56
KUSHANS 26, 41, 46
KYRGYZ 30, 60, 67
KYRGYZSTAN 33–34